Ready to Pray
A Workbook

A Spiritual Journey of
Prayer and Worship

Gail E. Dudley

Editing

Stephanie Bright-Mayberry
Bright Ideas Creative Design and Consulting

Copyediting and Interior Page Formatting

Kathy Curtis
Website: www.christianbookformat.com
E-mail: www.christianbookformat@gmail.com

Published by Gail E. Dudley
Website: www.GailDudley.com
Highly Recommended International, Inc.
Ministry In Motion Ministries International
The Church at North Pointe
www.GetRealLife.net
Columbus, Ohio
United States of America
614-441-8178
E-mail: GED@MIMToday.org

PROCLAMATION

S econd Chronicles 7:14-15 speaks to us clearly and with
great power what the Lord desires for our lives:

> *"if my people, who are called by my name, will humble them-*
> *selves and pray and seek my face and turn from their wicked*
> *ways, then will I hear from heaven and will forgive their sin*
> *and will heal their land. Now my eyes will be open and my*
> *ears attentive to the prayers offered in this place."*

I declare and decree in the name of Jesus that your
prayer life will change and be focused on the will of
the Lord. I pray that you will pray prayers of life, healing, deliverance, strength, and wisdom, and pray for
individuals without Christ you will speak with a special anointing: "Every knee shall bow and every tongue
confess that Jesus Christ is Lord." I pray from this day
forward that you step out in faith and live as God, our
Father in Heaven, has ordained you to live.

In Obedience to Christ,

FOREWORD

When I sit down to read a book, I usually grab pen and paper so that I can jot down notes as I read. Occasionally I remember to keep my notes with the book, but more times than not, I misplace the notes and lose the momentum of those thoughts. I was excited to learn that Gail was publishing a workbook, *Ready to Pray*, to go along with her book by the same title. Not only will the reader be able to work through the Scriptures and principles that Gail teaches, but they will also have a place to keep their notes for future reference.

In the *Ready to Pray* workbook, Gail provides an opportunity for the reader to search through Scripture and "dig on their own" to find answers regarding the importance of prayer, the results of prayer, the outcome of prayer, the meaning of prayer, and the spiritual growth that comes through prayer. She also provides opportunities for the reader to reflect on Scripture and to journal their insight. (2 Timothy 2:7) In addition, Gail provides thought-provoking questions that help the reader apply Scripture and Biblical principles to their prayer life today.

As you progress through this workbook, *Ready to Pray*, jot your notes in the margin, highlight the Scriptures that speak to your heart, and be confident of two things: First, the Holy Spirit guides your reading and gives understanding to your mind and your heart; second, you won't have to worry about losing your notes because they are all in this wonderful, compact workbook that Gail had the foresight to put together just for you!

Enjoy.

Mary Hamrick
Dragonfly Ministries
www.dragonflyministries.com

A PRAYER OF THANKS

Praise God for His hand of favor to allow me to complete this "Prayer Project." It's been three long years of seeking His face as to the direction I was to take during this journey. Many times I thought this project was completed to find that He brought it to a halt only to speak life in a more powerful way. He led me to truly listen to others and their challenges and fears of prayer. He caused me to go through some things—things where I wanted to simply walk away from ministry as a whole in order to write more clearly on prayer. He allowed me to enlarge my tent, lengthen my cords, and strengthen my stakes. (Isaiah 54:2) Thank you, God, for never leaving me nor forsaking me and for challenging me to go deeper in understanding our relationship. You do love me. Thank you!

To the Sisters of the Word (SOW) of The Church at North Pointe: Thank you for allowing me to speak into your life on a weekly basis. Thank you for praying for me and for holding me accountable. Thank you for pushing me. Thank you for being one of my biggest cheerleaders.

To the partners at The Church at North Pointe: Thank you. Weekly you avail yourselves and allow me to speak a word of prayer into your spirits. You allow me to step in when Pastor is away and you treat me like family. Thank you for all the times I hear the Lord speak "Prayer Gathering" and you come and sit with me for twenty-four hours in prayer. You are truly a blessing.

Stephanie Bright-Mayberry: Thank you! I love you girl!!! You have made this project much easier by being an excellent editor and a patient one at that! Sister, you stayed up many nights after being mommy to three beautiful girls and wife to your husband. In the face of many life challenges, you still took time out to walk with me on this journey to complete this project.

Mom and Dad, thank you for teaching me to pray at an early age. It prepared me for the journey I am currently walking.

Dominiq and Alexander, there is nothing that can bring me joy like hearing your laughter as I plug away typing these pages throughout this workbook. You gave me great material to use just by the realization that God allowed me to bring forth life in another.

To my boyfriend, my husband, my best friend; thank you for speaking truth to me time and time again. Many times I did not want to hear the truth but the truth you spoke reminded me that "Truth will set me free." You are my life companion. I know I have worked your last nerve but you still love me unconditionally. What a man! You believe in me and that means more to me than words can express. I love you – I love you much!

A Prayer for You

Under the Shadow of the Most High God; that is where we can rest. "Be still and know…"

Let us pray.

Most Holy and Awesome God, how excellent is Your name in all the earth—the God of peace, love, power, and gentleness, who sits high and looks low and rains showers of blessings and favor. In the name of Jesus, I pray for the person reading this right now. Lord, if it be Thy will, bless their family, their neighbors, their friends, their coworkers, and even their enemies. Father, only You know exactly each person's personal and corporate needs. Jesus, we lift up Your name, first and foremost. Then we lift up every concern, every dream, every desire, every challenge, in this moment. Breathe into Your servant new life. May they find rest in the shadow of the Almighty God! Open up the windows of heaven and pour unto them a blessing that they will not have room enough to receive.

We join and stand in agreement with what is prayed by the apostle Paul in Ephesians 3:14-19: "For this reason I kneel before the Father, from whom His whole family in heaven and on earth derives its name. I pray that out of His glorious riches He may strengthen you with power through His Spirit in your inner being, so that Christ may dwell in your hearts through faith. And I pray that you, being rooted and established in love, may have power, together with all the saints, to grasp how wide and long and high and deep is the love of Christ, and to know this love that surpasses knowledge that you may be filled to the measure of all the fullness of God."

In the name of Jesus, I speak life to each reader and student of prayer. I pray your guidance, obedience, direction, a fresh anointing, an increase in your discernment, encouragement, boldness, and opportunities to minister and to pray alongside and with others as the Spirit of the Lord leads. I pray your life to be strengthened by the power of the Holy Spirit. I pray the blood of Jesus upon and within your life. I pray that you are stretched in an unusual way and that your faith is strengthened in Christ. I pray your life will overflow with abundance of the grace of the Lord. I pray the many gifts God has placed on the inside of you are stirred to move you to another level in Him during this new season in your life. I declare and decree that you will be a lender and not a borrower in the name of Jesus. I declare that you are blessed in the city and blessed in the field. I pray that you will bear much fruit in all that you put your hands to. I speak abundance, knowledge, and wisdom. I pray your prosperity in the Word of the Lord. I pray for ministry resources and thank You, Lord, in advance for manifesting Your Word and Your presence in our lives according to 3 John 2: "Beloved, I wish above all things that thou mayest prosper and be in health, even as thy soul prospereth."

In the mighty and precious, most powerful name of Jesus — AMEN!

CONTENTS

INTRODUCTION AND INSTRUCTIONS

Why this workbook? Why another book on prayer? What will this book on prayer say differently than the million and one other workbooks on prayer that line the shelves across the nations?

Even the Bible gives us the instructions to pray. Isn't that all we need? The Bible says, "But thou, when thou prayest, enter into thy closet, and when thou hast shut thy door, pray to thy Father which is in secret; and thy Father which seeth in secret shall reward thee openly. But when ye pray, use not vain repetitions, as the heathen do: for they think that they shall be heard for their much speaking. Be not ye therefore like unto them: for your Father knoweth what things ye have need of, before ye ask him. After this manner therefore pray ye: Our Father which art in heaven, Hallowed by thy name. Thy kingdom come. Thy will be done in earth, as it is in heaven. Give us this day our daily bread. And forgive us our debts, as we forgive our debtors. And lead us not into temptation, but deliver us from evil: For thine is the kingdom, and the power, and the glory, forever. Amen." (Matthew 6:6-13 KJV)

And yet, here's another book on prayer. This workbook for prayer can be used to guide you in seeking God's vision for your personal and corporate prayer time.

Yes, I realize we each have taken a journey and I would like to share with you, through this hands-on workbook, my journey of prayer and worship. Not that I am expert, for I am not, but God has gifted me with an understanding on how to pray in everyday life situations.

In 2005 I prayed, for the first time in my life, and actually meant it: "Thy will be done." What was the life situation that brought me to that point in my life? To put it simply, there was nowhere else to turn and no one else to turn to. It was time to "pray and believe God." Did my situation turn around quickly? No. However, it was the relationship I developed with Christ through prayer and fasting that made all the difference in my life and now, today, I am instructed to share these tools with you.

Praying purpose is praying Ephesians 3:14-21. When you pray, "For this reason...," insert the reason — whatever it is.

Living a life of prayer and intercession allows one to stand in the gap for another person. This prayer workbook is a guide to assist you in developing a personal life of intercession and assembling a team of intercessors in your church, community, home, workplace, networking groups, etc. Listed below are a few suggestions to get you started:

- Establish a team of prayer warriors and pray as the Lord leads. Pray His heart.
- When you come in contact with others, ask, "How may I pray for you today?"
- As you are driving, walking, exercising, or sitting in a restaurant, silently pray for individuals you pass by or who may pass by you to know the Lord. Pray for their healing. Pray for their anointing. Pray for their protection and so on.
- Send a text message, write a note to someone and share a word or verse that encouraged you that day.
- Text a brief prayer to your contact list once per week.
- Pray a silent prayer when someone crosses your mind. Pray a silent prayer as you review your caller ID prior to answering your telephone.
- When you drive past a car accident, pray.

As you go through this workbook, I encourage you to have a few tools at hand. Use this book to the full extent: write in it, carry it with you, and let your journey with *Ready To Pray* change your prayer life. Below are some suggestions to be used along with your workbook as you go on your journey.

- Have a study Bible you can write in, write on, and mark up.

- Get a prayer journal.
- Go through your Bible and find all the prayer Scriptures you can find.
- Have a set time to fast and to pray.
- Ask the Lord to connect you with a committed prayer partner.

I

Ready to Pray

"Prayer is when we go to God with our heart
and come away with His."
– unknown

I must say that I laugh when I hear people freely say, "Let's pray." "Pray about what?" I want to shout! It's a common phrase we simply say when we hear someone going through a tough time or when we experience an uncommon situation. The moment someone shares, there's a moment of silence and then without fail someone says it, "Let's Pray!"

"Let's pray." Do we really understand what we are saying? We respond or share what we have witnessed in the past without having a real relationship or understanding of what is needed. We begin to proclaim and start decreeing and declaring without even knowing what we are really praying about. People are sincere and have a mind to want to encourage people and to pray for one another, but my concern is that we say, "I'll pray for you," only to walk away and never actually pray. This happens because we really don't know what to pray or how to pray. Other times we are simply uncomfortable in praying because we have not developed an intimate relationship with Christ. It's difficult to engage in an ongoing conversation without establishing some sort of relationship.

God has revealed to us through His Word over and over again who He is. Below are some Scriptures that may be found in the following Books of the Bible (New International Version):

- Deuteronomy 4:29: "But if from there you seek the Lord your God, you will find him if you look for him with all your heart and with all your soul."
- Genesis 35:11: "And God said to him, "I am God Almighty...."
- Genesis 46:3: "'I am God, the God of your father,' he said."
- Exodus 3:14: "God said to Moses, 'I AM WHO I AM.'"
- Hosea 10:12: "Sow for yourselves righteousness, reap the fruit of unfailing love, and break up your unplowed ground; for it is time to seek the Lord, until he comes and showers righteousness on you."
- Psalms 42:1, 2: "As the deer pants for streams of water, so my soul pants for you, O God. My soul

thirsts for God, for the living God. When can I go and meet with God?"

God is always available to meet and to share in conversation with all of His children. He will visit us whenever we invite Him. It's about seeking Him and inviting Him. It's saying, "Come, Lord Jesus."
When we pray:

- We must know who Jesus is.
  Revelation 1:8 says, "'I am the Alpha and the Omega,' says the Lord God, 'who is, and who was, and who is to come, the Almighty.'"

- We must invite Him to come in.
  Revelation 3:20 says, "Here I am! I stand at the door and knock. If anyone hears my voice and opens the door, I will come in and eat with him, and he with me."

- We must come to God with our heart.
  We must seek His face — we acknowledge Christ — and call out to Him, "Abba Father!" It's about praying the Lord's heart and praying what He desires. When our heart is lined up with His heart and when we give of ourselves totally to God, we pray what He desires us to pray.

You are able to pray His heart when you are able to wrap your mind around this example.

First, think about a symphony orchestra. The most important person in an orchestra — the conductor — does not play an instrument at all. The conductor's job, at its most basic level, is to indicate the beat of the music. The conductor uses a baton to instruct the entire orchestra. With each movement of the baton, the conductor is instructing with imaginary points that indicate the beat in the bar the orchestra is playing. Think about Jesus. He is the most important person during your conversation. When your heartbeat begins to line up with His heartbeat, you will find yourself praying what He is praying. "Thy kingdom come, thy will be done...." You are now praying what He desires you to pray. You are now focused on His thoughts and His will and His direction and find that your thoughts are no longer as important as before. Your mind is now focused on Christ Jesus.

When you are falling in love with Jesus and becoming more intimate with Him through prayer, you will learn His voice. As the conductor, Christ will prepare you. You see, the conductor's role in the orchestra is being responsible for the preparation, the rehearsal, and for making interpretative decisions, such as whether a certain passage should be slow, fast, soft, loud, smooth, aggressive, and so forth. Ah, and also so it is with Jesus. He will speak to you boldly, compassionately, through a whisper, and will instruct you to be obedient. Through the reading of

His Word, you will know to wait patiently, move swiftly, to be still, and so on.

A conductor of an orchestra communicates their decisions both verbally during the rehearsal and during the performance, using different movements, gestures, and expressions. During prayer, you will know what Jesus is communicating with you because you have spent time with Him. You have become more intimate with Him and your heartbeat is now beating with His.

Next, think only about the symphony. There are usually four movements to a symphony. A *sonata*, from the Italian word meaning "to sound," often is the first movement, sometimes referred to as "sonata form" or "first-movement form." Our prayers should be based upon the conductor, Jesus Christ, and be in concert with Him through intercession.

With a typical symphony, the first movement is a fairly fast movement, weighty in content and feeling. That's where we get the "sonata form." Looking at prayer, when we begin to pray and spend time with the Lord, we are usually in a hurry. We rush through our time with Him because we don't always know what to expect.

The second movement of a symphony will be slow and solemn in character. As we pray, we may find the second time around to be quieter, slower. The pounding of the heart slows down. There's room for silence—you may no longer be in a hurry. You have decided to take your time and watch and pray.

The third movement of a symphony can be inter-changed with the second movement. When we pray, we may find ourselves in a hurry in the beginning but, later, get with God and slow down because we are finally rest-ing in His arms.

The fourth movement in a symphony creates the finale. The finale is made up of a variation. A variation movement consists of a theme, usually made up of four- or eight-bar phrases in which the theme is elaborated, developed, and transformed.

Although a symphony may seem difficult in our natu-ral hearing, it's easy to those who are a part of the orches-tra. With Christ, we may think this journey of prayer and worship is difficult, but it's a beautiful journey once we line up with Christ as the focus of our time in interces-sion and prayer with Him.

- Once we are in concert with Jesus Christ, we move into intercession.
- When we pray, even in our weakness, the Holy Spirit is present. Romans 8:26 says, "In the same way, the Spirit helps us in our weakness. We do not know what we ought to pray for, but the Spirit himself intercedes for us with groans that words cannot express."

In randomly interviewing Christians over a one-year period, I found that one out of every three people shared that they do not pray because they have no idea what to pray for or how to pray. Have you felt as though you cannot pray because you do not know what to say? Please explain your answer. _____

_____

_____

_____

_____

_____

I have listed throughout this section and throughout this workbook many suggested Bible verses pertaining to prayer. However, in the next few pages, I would like to highlight Scriptures that speak to the importance on seeking the face of Christ and keeping God at the center of all of your prayers. It is very easy to pray what you want and to pray what your flesh is speaking, but may I encourage you to keep Christ at the center of your prayers. Remain in the Bible and meditate on the Scriptures, both day and night. Study the Word of the Lord, for the Bible says, "Study to show thyself approved unto God, a workman that needeth not to be ashamed, rightly dividing the word of truth." (2 Timothy 2:15 KJV)

There are many Scriptures in the Bible that speak on and encourage prayer. However, I would like to highlight three particular Scriptures. I am not saying that these three are more important than the others, for all Scripture is equally important and very beneficial to your prayer life. I list the following three Scriptures so that we can work our way through the basics of prayer.

- "If my people, who are called by my name, will humble themselves and pray and seek my face and turn from their wicked ways, then will I hear from heaven and will forgive their sin and will heal their land. Now my eyes will be open and my ears attentive to the prayers offered in this place." (2 Chronicles 7:14-15 NIV)

- "Call to me and I will answer you and tell you great and unsearchable things you do not know." (Jeremiah 33:3 NIV)

- "Could you not keep watch for one hour? Watch and pray so that you will not fall into temptation. The spirit is willing, but the body is weak." (Mark 14:37b-38 NIV)

Let's start with 2 Chronicles 7:14-15.

- What is God speaking?
  (NOTE: You will see this question asked through-out the prayer workbook over and over again. We never want to move in our own strength or our own desires but that of the strength and the desires and voice of the Holy One.)

So again, "What is God speaking?" Please explain.

_____

_____

_____

_____

- How do we humble ourselves? Can one ever become too humbled? Explain.

_____

_____

_____

_____

- When will the land be healed? Think and pray about your answer.

_____

_____

_____

_____

_____

- What will your eyes be opened to and what do you do with what you see?

_____

_____

_____

_____

Next, let's revisit, Jeremiah 33:3.

- How should we call upon the Lord? What does that look like? What does calling unto the Lord really mean? Please explain.

  _____

  _____

  _____

  _____

  _____

  _____

- What is God going to tell us? Are you ready for what you may not know?

  _____

  _____

  _____

  _____

  _____

  _____

- What will be our responsibility once we are made aware of the unknown?

  _____

  _____

  _____

  _____

  _____

Finally, let's look at Mark 14:37b-38.

- Why is it difficult to watch and pray for one hour?

  _____
  _____
  _____
  _____
  _____
  _____
  _____

- Does God really mean one full hour? Please explain.

  _____
  _____
  _____
  _____
  _____

- Is your spirit willing? If your answer is yes, then what is the "fight" about?

  _____
  _____
  _____
  _____
  _____

- One more question. Can God trust you to pray? Explain your answer.

_____

_____

_____

_____

_____

_____

As we approach God, we want to come to Him:

- Emptied and Available
- to have our hearts examined by God
- to receive truth from God
- to hear clearly the voice of God
- as you sit waiting in anticipation for God's answers; and
- to walk in the confidence and obedience of Christ.
- Intentional
- Start with being deliberate about searching Scriptures to keep you and your prayers focused on Christ.
- Lining your heart up with the heart of Christ.

In prayer, we are becoming more intimate with Jesus. The more time we sit at the feet of Jesus and drink from the fountain of living water, the more intimately connected we become. Looking at John 7:37-38, we read "...If anyone is thirsty, let him come to me and drink. Whoever believes in me, as the Scripture has said, streams of living water will flow from within him." Remember the woman at the well? John 4:13-15 says, "Jesus answered, 'Everyone who drinks this water will be thirsty again, but whoever drinks the water I give him will never thirst. Indeed, the water I give him will become in him a spring of water welling up to eternal life.' The woman said to him, 'Sir, give me this water so that I won't get thirsty and have to keep coming here to draw water.'"

Are you thirsty? Why not drink from the well of living water of Jesus.

NOTES:

_____

_____

_____

_____

_____

_____

_____

_____

_____

_____

_____

_____

_____

_____

_____

_____

_____

_____

_____

_____

_____

_____

_____

_____

_____

_____

II

WHEN YOU PRAY

When you are praying purposefully:

- **Pray the details.** Be specific in your prayers.
- **Pray expecting God to answer—His will, not yours.**
- **Ask yourself, "Do I really expect my prayers to be answered by God?"**
- **Know the Scriptures.** Study the Bible and write in a journal all Scriptures that reference prayer. Ask yourself, "What is God speaking?" Write what is on your heart.
- **Pray prayers of being thankful, petition, confession, praise, and intercession.**
- **Keep a prayer journal:** Write out prayer requests and the praise report or updates.
- **Be honest:** Pray with an honest heart. Tell God what's really going on with you. Yes, He already

knows, but share with Him the truth. Always operate in the truth.

- **Be determined:** Jesus told the parable of praying and never giving up. He talks about the widow and the judge. She was determined. (Luke 18:1-5) Also, think about the man who knocks continuously until his friend gets out of bed to answer his request. Again in the Bible, Jesus said to ask, seek, and knock — a continuous asking, seeking, and knocking (see Luke 11:8-10).

- **Stand in agreement:** Seek God for a prayer partner or a prayer team. I have a team of prayer warriors to pray with me and for me. Sometimes it is to stand in agreement and at other times it is to cover me in prayer. Jesus gave a model for prayers of agreement (see Matthew 18:19-20).

- **Pray the Scriptures:** Pray in accordance with God's will. Find a Scripture to pray for concerns.

- **Allow the Holy Spirit to move:** The Bible says in Romans 8:26-27, "In the same way, the Spirit helps us in our weakness. We do not know what we ought to pray for, but the Spirit himself intercedes for us with groans that words cannot express. And he who searches our hearts knows the mind of the Spirit, because the Spirit intercedes for the saints in accordance with God's will." Whatever we are faced with, our circumstance or crisis, when we invite the Holy Spirit to pray through us, we begin to pray the will of the Lord. Try not to pray the problem—pray as the Holy Spirit leads. Never assume God is going to answer based upon what you want or within your exact time frame. Try not to box God in based upon your selfish desires, needs, and expectations.

- **Have an attitude of thanks:** Go to God in prayer with requests of thanksgiving. Tell God how much you appreciate Him. Be thankful, thanking in advance for answers to your prayers based upon His will. (Philippians 4:6)
- **Set time aside to fast and pray**: Spend time alone with God. Seek Him without food, television, telephone, the computer, and the everyday distractions of life. Seek God for directions and His answers to your prayers.
- **Give God praise**: "I will bless the Lord at all times; His praise shall continually be in my mouth." (Psalm 34:1) He is enthroned in the praises of His people. (Psalm 22:3)
- **Believe God and trust Him—always**: "Trust in the Lord with all your heart and lean not unto your own understanding." (Proverbs 3:5) You and me, we do not have the power. "...For we have no power to face this vast army that is attacking us. We do not know what to do, but our eyes are upon you." (2 Chronicles 20:12)

Before you pray...

1. Believe. Deal with any unbelief that you may have.
2. Forgive. Make sure there is no unforgiveness in your heart.
3. Confess. Go to God with any unconfessed sin.

Jesus says in Mark 11:24-25: "Therefore I tell you, whatever you ask for in prayer, believe that you have received it, and it will be yours. And when you stand praying, if you hold anything against anyone, forgive him, so that your Father in heaven may forgive you your sins."

NOTES:

_____

_____

_____

_____

_____

_____

_____

_____

_____

_____

_____

_____

_____

_____

_____

_____

_____

_____

_____

_____

_____

_____

_____

_____

_____

_____

III

PRAYING WITH A PURPOSE

Study Objectives: To discover the importance and benefit of knowing God and to learn how to experience the Lord personally through the power of prayer.

Scripture References:

- Acts 16:25-31
- Luke 11:1-13
- Ephesians 3:14-19
- Matthew 26:36

Why Pray?

- No matter what Jesus did — He made prayer His priority.
  - Why pray? Jesus is a prime example of a life lived by prayer that offers relevance, purpose, answers, and most of all, a relationship

with God, the Father. Jesus prayed whole-heartedly for every move He made, asking God for guidance, leading, and direction. He prayed prayers of thanks, prayers for healing, prayers for His disciples, and prayers for believers — present and future.

- Prayer not only establishes a relationship with God, it is also vital to maintaining our relationship with Him.
- Prayer helps us focus on God.
    - Time spent with God in prayer deepens our knowledge of and relationship with Him.
    - Through prayer:
        - We acknowledge our dependence on Him.
        - We invite Him to take control of our life situations.
        - We seek His will.
        - We give Him an opportunity to demonstrate His power.
        - We bring glory to God.
        - We are freed from worry.
            - It may not change the situation or circumstance. However, once you have prayed you see things differently (if we trust Him).
            - We can access His supernatural power (James 5:16)

What Is Prayer?

Prayer should be the most natural thing in the world, like speaking your mind with a friend you trust. C. Neil Strait said, "Prayer is...talking with God and telling Him you love Him—it is conversing with God about all the things that are important in life, both large and small, and being assured that He is listening."

- Prayer is talking to your Father in heaven and getting to know Him.
- It's the process of developing a relationship.
- Prayer is seeking direction from God.
- Prayer is recognizing who God is and offering Him glory, honor, and adoration.
- Prayer is personal.
- Prayer is intimate.
- Prayer is a conversation.
- Prayer is real; authentic; genuine.
- Prayer is expressive.
- It is having an intimate relationship with Christ and knowing who He is.

He is:

El Shaddai — The All-Sufficient One
El Elyon — The Most High God
Jehovah-Nissi — The Lord my Banner
Elohim — The Creator
Jehovah-Shalom — The Lord my Peace
Jehovah-Jireh — The Lord my Provider
Jehovah-Raah — The Lord is my Shepherd
Jehovah-Shammah — The Lord is There
Jehovah-Tsidkenu — The Lord our Righteousness
Yahweh — Lord (Jehovah)
Adonai — Lord, Master
El Roi — The God who Sees

"Those who know your name will trust in you, for you, Lord, have never forsaken those who seek you."
Psalm 9:10

Instructions for Prayer

- Prayer is a partnership with God.
- Prayer is living in the name of Jesus.
  (Luke 11:1-13)

Patterns of Prayer

(Matthew 6:5-15)

Praise:

"Hallowed by Your name" "Yours is the glory"
- *The prayer begins in an attitude of worship, acknowledging our relationship with God as our heavenly Father and honoring His holy name.*

Participation:

"Your kingdom come" "Your will be done on earth"
- *It expresses a desire for God's will (whatever His will may be in our lives).*

"As we forgive those" "AMEN"
- *We must freely extend our forgiveness to those who have wronged us.*

Petition:

"Give us this day" "Deliver us from evil"
- *We are to ask God to provide our everyday needs.*
- *We seek God's wisdom, guidance, and protection each day to help us do what is right and keep us from sin.*

Penitence (repentance, apology):

"Forgive us"
- *As we confess our sins and receive God's forgiveness*

Profession:

"This is the power"
- *We thank and praise God for His power, majesty, and strength, and for the fact that He is in control!*

Approaches to Prayer

- Person-driven
- Issue-driven
- Scripture-directed
- Spirit-directed

How to Pray

John 16:23 says, "In that day you will no longer ask me anything. I tell you the truth, my Father will give you whatever you ask in my name." vs. 24: "Until now you have not asked for anything in my name. Ask and you will receive, and your joy will be complete." vs. 26: "...I am not saying that I will ask the Father on your behalf. No, the Father himself loves you because you have loved me and have believed...."

- Pray with love
- Pray believing

Praying in Jesus' name means praying for a request as Jesus would pray for it. It shows our desire to align our interest, our mind, and our will with His. It indicates our belief and trust in Him.

Therefore, we should pray...

Regularly (Luke 18:1)
Confidently (Hebrews 4:16)
Patiently (Psalm 37:7)
Simply (Luke 18:38)
Continually (1 Thessalonians 5:17)
Expectantly (John 14:11-14)
Dependently (Romans 8:26-27)
Righteously (1 Peter 3:17)
Persistently (Matthew 7:7-8)
Honestly (Psalm 139)
Thankfully (Philippians 4:6-7)
Intentionally (James 4:8)
Spiritually (Ephesians 6:18)
Sincerely (Matthew 6:5-6)
Faithfully (Ephesians 3:12)

NOTES:

IV

Praying God's Word

Want to pray effectively? Add power to your prayers by praying God's Word.

Yield to God's Word when you begin to pray. There was a moment in my Christian walk when I experienced an urgency to pray the Word of the Lord rather than fumbling with my natural words during prayer. I used to use fillers to extend my prayers. Why? Because I really didn't know what to say or what to pray. I wanted to sound like the person I heard during church service. They had such a powerful praying voice and their prayer extended for more than a couple of minutes. I began to mimic what I heard from others and became phony in my prayers instead of seeking God for myself and praying what He led me to pray.

Have you been in this place—the place of mimicking others? Tell the truth. Write out what you have mimicked.

_____

_____

_____

Did you feel as though your prayer fell flat on its face? Explain.

_____

_____

_____

_____

Once you realized that God wanted you to be true in your communication with and about Him, how did your prayers change?

_____

_____

_____

_____

_____

_____

_____

When I decided to seek Him for myself instead of following the walk of someone else, God began to show me "what not to do." I sat one day in amazement when I listened intensely to a conversation of believers. I noticed a common phrase which seemed to roll off the tongue with such ease: "In the name of Jesus." Sitting in this environment for a couple of hours, I heard over and over again, "In the name of Jesus." For whatever reason, God was speaking to me to pay close attention.

Weeks later while driving and talking on my cell phone with a friend, she found herself going the wrong direction and she immediately said, "In the name of Jesus, allow me to turn around and go in the right direction." I laughed to myself and said, "There's that common phrase with Christians." I then asked my friend, "Will turning around in the middle of the street cause an illegal action?" (I will not tell you what she said). It did get me thinking; do we take Jesus for granted? Do we think He is some magical being that if we say, "In the name of Jesus" so naturally that we don't have to follow any rules and we get our way? Yes, there is power in the name of Jesus but we must not abuse and misuse His name. Think about it for a moment.

How often do you say, "In the name of Jesus"? _____

_____

_____

Why are you saying, "In the name of Jesus"? _____

_____

_____

_____

_____

_____

Do you really want to see a move of God in calling on His name? _____

_____

_____

_____

Please do not misunderstand me. Yes, we should call on His name. However, I want to challenge you to think about when you call on Him. He's already with us, right? *I'll let you think about that for a moment.*

If God is with us, and He is, why do we pray every chance we get "In the name of Jesus?"

_____

_____

_____

_____

_____

_____

Is this simply a habit that we have formed? Are we using His name for something magical? Explain.

_____

_____

_____

_____

_____

Do you really believe that "In the name of Jesus" will change your life or the life of another as you pray? If so, why do you believe it does?

_____

_____

_____

_____

_____

How many Scriptures can you find throughout the Bible where one prayed by saying, "In the name of Jesus"? Please list them. _____

_____

_____

_____

_____

_____

_____

_____

_____

Let me assist you.

"Do not stop him," **Jesus** said. "No one who does a miracle in my **name**...." (Mark 9:39)

"**Jesus** answered, 'I did tell you, but you do not believe. The miracles I do in my Father's **name** speak for me....'" (John 10:25)

"Peter replied, 'Repent and be baptized, every one of you, in the **name** of **Jesus** Christ for the forgiveness of your sins. And you will receive the gift of the Holy Spirit.'" (Acts 2:38)

"Then Peter said, 'Silver or gold I do not have, but what I have I give you. In the **name** of **Jesus** Christ of Nazareth, walk.'" (Acts 3:6)

"Stretch out your hand to heal and perform miraculous signs and wonders through the **name** of your holy servant **Jesus**." (Acts 4:30)

There's more—I just wanted to get you started.

Please take note of when and why Jesus' name was declared.

What's the difference when they called on His name in the Holy Scriptures compared to when we call on His name today? Write about it. _____

_____

_____

_____

_____

_____

_____

_____

_____

Well then, why don't we pray God's Word? _____

_____

_____

_____

_____

_____

_____

The Word of the Lord is powerful and mighty. Could you imagine if we simply prayed the Word of the Lord? The Bible says, "At the name of Jesus, every knee shall bow and tongue shall confess that Jesus is Lord." (Romans 14:11) There are two things God honors: His name and His Word. Praying God's Word results in powerful prayer. The Bible says in Hebrews 4:12, "For the word of God is full of living power. It is sharper than the sharpest knife, cutting deep into our innermost thoughts and desires." When we pray God's Word, His will — will be done! God's Word is living. God's Word is life. God's Word is active. God's Word is power. Praying God's Word gives strength and power to our prayers.

How then shall you pray God's Word? _____

_____

_____

_____

In order to pray God's Word, one must stay in the Bible, studying both day and night. I honestly believe God is pleased when we study His Word and pray His Word. It shows Him that we take His Word seriously. It shows Him that we seek Him and His Will and His heart. It says that we want to know Him and the beauty of His holiness. We are praying, "Thy Will be done" because we believe Him. We're praying what He wants us to pray. It communicates to God that we want our will to line up with His will and His promises for our life. By praying the Scriptures, the Word of the Lord adds power to our prayer and adds delight to His heart.

NOTES:

_____

_____

_____

_____

_____

_____

_____

_____

_____

_____

_____

_____

_____

_____

_____

_____

_____

_____

_____

_____

_____

_____

_____

_____

_____

_____

V

MORE THAN WORDS

"But when you pray, go into your room,
close the door and pray to your Father, who is unseen.
Then your Father, who sees what is done in secret,
will reward you."
Matthew 6:6 NIV

Remember the index cards we used and our so-called "Cliff Notes," those short and handy little summary note cards that we used as our study guide or the very thing we use to give a speech? When it comes to understanding prayer, Jesus laid out everything you need to know in Matthew: step-by-step details on how to pray, how not to pray, and the essentials of forgiveness.

Today, take a moment right where you sit reading this devotional, pick up your sword, the Word of the Lord, in the beginning of Matthew 6, and read what Jesus had to say about prayer.

In Matthew 6:7 we read, "And when you pray, do not keep on babbling like pagans, for they think they will be heard because of their many words."

So, you are not so good with words. You get all tongue-tied when you're trying to speak from your heart. Maybe you are great with words and speak with ease and the words simply roll off your tongue with grace. Either way, it doesn't matter when it comes to prayer. God is not looking for long words, words you cannot pronounce, or flowery words. The Lord our God wants to have simple, honest conversation with you. Simply say what's on your heart.

Sit down with Him and have a conversation. Imagine sitting across the table from Jesus, sharing your heart. Take a sip of your tea, lean forward, and rest in the shadow of the Almighty God. Speak, and then listen. Be still and know that He is God.

What does Jesus have to say about prayer? _____

_____

_____

_____

_____

_____

_____

_____

_____

_____

Write out your personal prayer here. Write something simple, yet real and authentic. _____

_____

_____

_____

_____

_____

_____

_____

_____

_____

_____

_____

_____

_____

_____

_____

_____

_____

_____

_____

_____

_____

_____

_____

NOTES:

_____

_____

_____

_____

_____

_____

_____

_____

_____

_____

_____

_____

_____

_____

_____

_____

_____

_____

_____

_____

_____

_____

_____

_____

_____

_____

_____

_____

VI

I Am Praying for You

"I urge, then, first of all, that requests, prayers,
intercession and thanksgiving be made for everyone."
1 Timothy 2:1

In our culture today, the intentional prayer of the
believers is absolutely critical if we are to see any real
change in the lives of people who so desperately need
the presence of Christ.

How can we be more intentional in our prayer life?

_____

_____

_____

_____

_____

_____

_____

_____

- Prayer is an intimate relationship with God.
- Prayer is speaking a love language from our lips to God's ears.
- Prayer is seeking God on behalf of others.

How do you connect with the heart of God? _____

_____

_____

_____

_____

_____

_____

_____

How can you uncover ways to become more compassionate and committed to a lifestyle of effective prayer?

_____

_____

_____

_____

_____

_____

_____

_____

_____

_____

NOTES:

VII

YEARNING FOR GOD

To yearn is to desire, to long, to hunger, to thirst for.

Scripture References:

- "I myself will see him with my own eyes—I, and not another. How my heart yearns within me!" (Job 19:27)

- "How lovely is your dwelling place, O Lord Almighty. My soul yearns, even faints, for the courts of the Lord; my heart and my flesh cry out for the living God." (Psalm 84:1, 2)

- "My soul yearns for you in the night; in the morning my spirit longs for you." (Isaiah 26:9a)

I can recall a time when all I could do was think about God. Nothing I tried to do to fill the void left me satisfied.

It was an unusual thirst for God. I tried reading. It didn't work. I tried watching television. It didn't work. I tried talking on the telephone. It didn't work. There were many things I tried, but nothing worked. I had a yearning for the Lord that could only be filled with Christ Himself.

Have you ever longed for God? Explain. _____

_____

_____

_____

_____

_____

_____

Job 19:27 says, "I myself will see with my own eyes—I, and not another. How my heart yearns within me!" What does this Scripture say to you?

_____

_____

_____

_____

_____

_____

_____

Look at Psalm 84:1-2, particularly focusing on, "My soul yearns, even faints, for the courts of the Lord." How does this move in your spirit? Explain. _____

_____

_____

_____

_____

_____

When we read, "My soul yearns for you in the night; in the morning my spirit longs for you," why the difference of night and day? What is God speaking? _____

_____

_____

_____

_____

_____

_____

_____

_____

Proposition:

I hear the Lord calling us to come, be consecrated, set ourselves apart, and be with Him in a quiet place. Do you know the Lord desires us to spend time with Him? Quiet time. Alone time. A time of intimacy. One way of doing this is through fasting and prayer.

Fasting is having a heart that yearns (longs/hungers/thirsts) to become more intimate with Christ. Prayer is having an intimate conversation with God—when you go to God with your heart and you come away with His. The purpose of prayer is to have communication with God and for the availability of God to do God's will in the earth.

Thesis:

This is how it all begins. You decide to go on a fast. You are not sure why—you've heard that fasting is good for you because Daniel fasted. You decide to fast because the congregation you worship with is fasting. You've heard that Ash Wednesday (Lent season) is a time to begin to fast—so you fast. You are thinking a fast will help you to hear from the Lord. You may be thinking your fast will give you an opportunity to commune with God. You may begin with the right intentions, however, you get sidetracked. You begin to think, "Maybe I will drop a few pounds," "Maybe I will purge myself and clean my system," and the list goes on. Whatever the reason, I need to fast. I need to plan out my fast based upon my needs and the needs of my family; doing whatever I have to do to in order to make it in this game called life.

We exhaust ourselves in a mad dash to acquire the biggest, the best, and the most. (This is why many will fast—to receive something from Christ.) Before we know it, we get caught up in a never-ending spiral of fasting for all the wrong reasons. We have confused our wants and our needs with what God desires. We are consumed and now fast while being legalistic and hoping for something that is not real—a false relationship with Jesus. We are always reaching for more, for those things that are just beyond our grasp and often times use God instead of developing an authentic relationship with Him, longing for Him—a true relationship.

Do you wonder why fasting lasts only an hour or two for many people? It's as if we are about to compete and to prove something that is only between you and God in the first place. "On your mark...get set...FAST! You start your time of fasting prematurely. You have not prepared yourself for the fast. Your spirit is not settled and you are not sure why you started this fast in the first place. When you begin a twelve-hour fast, your main focus becomes the clock and not Christ. Something is off. Something is wrong. You are not fasting; you are dieting, or better yet, starting something that will bring you to a frustration of self instead of bringing you closer to God.

I've been here. I have said, "Tomorrow I will fast." Where did that come from? Did I make that up? Why am I fasting? Am I really looking for a day to cleanse my body? Right! Speaking truth—I've started a fast this way many times when I was immature in my walk with Christ. Yes, it was a start, but I was doing it for the wrong reasons. I'm thinking, "I may drop a couple of pounds today," but I end up eating more food in one hour than I ate the previous twenty-four hours.

Have you been there? Explain. _____

_____

_____

_____

_____

_____

_____

Antithesis:

"There are so many things I need answers to. " "I am seeking my purpose." " I am facing a financial challenge." " I need a new job." " I want a healthy marriage." " I want my children to make the right choices." " I want to live right." Okay, I'll go on a fast but I am not trying to do what Daniel did. I will go on a fast, but I need to change the fast.

Question:

Why do we fast? Are we to fast or not? What are the right reasons to fast? _____

_____

_____

What is fasting? Fasting is *not* going without food for a period of time. _____

_____

_____

_____

Synthesis:

- Seek Christ—Luke 2:36-38 NIV: "There was also a prophetess, Anna, the daughter of Phanuel, of the tribe of Asher. She was very old; she had lived with her husband seven years after her marriage, and then was a widow until she was eighty-four. She never left the temple but worshiped night and day, fasting and praying. Coming up to them at that very moment, she gave thanks to God and spoke about the child to all who were looking forward to the redemption of Jerusalem."

- Going Deeper—(Psalm 42:1-2a): "As a deer pants for streams of water, so my soul pants for you, O God." "My soul thirsts for God, for the living God."
    - o Fasting should bring one into a deeper, more intimate and powerful relationship with Christ.
    - o David's hunger and thirst for God was his focus, not his absence of food.

- Experiencing a Powerful Move of God
    - o A living sacrifice: (Romans 12:1) Offer your body to God as a living sacrifice.
    - o New Wine (Matthew 9:14-16 and Luke 5:33-39).
    - o Renewal.
    - o Be filled (John 7: 37-38).

Other Scripture References:

- Isaiah 58
- Daniel 1
- 2 Chronicles 15:2

NOTES:

_____

_____

_____

_____

_____

_____

_____

_____

_____

_____

_____

_____

_____

_____

_____

_____

_____

_____

_____

_____

_____

_____

_____

VIII

BE FILLED

Holy Spirit.

Old Testament—The Hebrew word for "Spirit" is *Ruwach*, meaning "wind" or "breath." The wind like the Spirit of God is unseen and active.

New Testament—The Greek word for "Spirit" is *Punuma*, which like the Hebrew word is derived from the meaning of wind or breath.

- The Holy Spirit is also called the Comforter or Helper.

What are your thoughts of how the Holy Spirit moves in your life? _____

_____

_____

_____

_____

_____

Have you experienced the Holy Spirit as Comforter or Helper? Please explain your answer. _____

_____

_____

_____

_____

_____

_____

_____

_____

_____

Scripture References:

- "All of them were filled with the Holy Spirit and began to speak in other tongues as the Spirit enabled them." *(Acts 2:4) Read Acts 2:1-13*

- "For it is we who are the circumcision, we who worship by the Spirit of God, who glory in Christ Jesus, and who put no confidence in the flesh...." *(Philippians 3:3)*

- "In him the whole building is joined together and rises to become a holy temple in the Lord. And in him you too are being built together to become a dwelling in which God lives by his Spirit. *(Ephesians 2:21, 22)*

After reading these Scriptures, how can you apply them in your life so that you experience the Holy Spirit daily?

_____

_____

_____

_____

_____

_____

_____

_____

_____

_____

_____

_____

_____

_____

_____

Proposition:

I want to be filled beyond satisfaction.

Watchman Nee said:

"Let us not forget that the greatest means of edification is not prayer, though that restores us; it is not reading the Word, though that refreshes us; it is not attending meetings and listening to the messages, though this does comfort and encourage us. The greatest means of edification is the discipline of the Holy Spirit in our lives. Like nothing else, this will build us up in strength to be able to minister to others."

— *Secrets to Spiritual Power*
(from the writings of Watchman Nee)
compiled by Sentinel Kulp,
Whitaker House, © 1998.

Looking over your life, how can you be filled beyond satisfaction? _____

_____

_____

_____

_____

_____

_____

_____

What's hindering you from being filled beyond satisfaction? Explain your answer. _____

_____

_____

_____

_____

_____

_____

_____

_____

Thesis:

Tired of running on empty? Oftentimes we try to satisfy ourselves with things that are only temporary. The Word of the Lord tells us in Acts 2:4: "All of them were filled with the Holy Spirit...." God, I want to be filled with thy Holy Spirit. Fill me.

List any fears you may have of being filled with the Holy Spirit. _____

_____

_____

_____

_____

_____

_____

What do you need to overcome your fears? _____

_____

_____

_____

_____

_____

_____

_____

_____

_____

Antithesis:

I want to be filled, but I am wondering what I have to give up in the process.

Do you really believe you have to give up anything in order to be filled? If so, explain. _____

_____

_____

_____

_____

_____

_____

_____

Question:

Where is the Holy Spirit? How can I be filled with the Holy Spirit? _____

_____

_____

_____

_____

_____

_____

_____

Synthesis:

- A desire to know Christ
  Philippians 3:10-11: "I want to know Christ and the power of his resurrection and the fellowship of sharing in his sufferings, becoming like him in his death, and so, somehow, to attain to the resurrection from the dead."
    - The work of the Holy Spirit is found wherever the resurrection power of the Lord is at work.
    - Express your desire (for the Holy Spirit to come upon you, you must express your desire) and He will come and fill you.

How will you know Christ? _____

_____

_____

_____

_____

_____

_____

_____

_____

- Receiving the Outpouring
    - Check your heart—deal with any sin within your heart.
    - Have a hunger, a thirst, a yearning in the spirit.
    - Pray a fervent prayer.
    - Receiving the outpouring is like an opened door—once it is opened....

Have you checked your heart lately? What do you see?

_____

_____

_____

_____

_____

_____

_____

- The Holy Spirit dwells.
  - The Holy Spirit gives people life.
  - The Holy Spirit dwells in you as life.
  - The Holy Spirit falls upon His people as power.
  - Be filled (John 7: 37-39)

"He who dwells in the secret place..."*(Psalm 91)* Where do you dwell? _____

_____

_____

_____

_____

_____

Other Scripture References:

- Acts 2:14-21

Read this passage of Acts and spend some time considering. Write what the Lord reveals to you. _____

_____

_____

_____

_____

_____

_____

NOTES:

_____

_____

_____

_____

_____

_____

_____

_____

_____

_____

_____

_____

_____

_____

_____

_____

_____

_____

_____

_____

_____

_____

_____

_____

_____

_____

IX

FASTING AND PRAYER

The Daniel Fast – Daniel 10:2-11

- Daniel mourned, consecrated himself, or partially fasted over the plight of his people, Israel. This can be noted in Daniel 10:2-11. We are mourning, consecrating ourselves, or partially fasting over the plight of our local church and local church family, world, nation, state, city, area, universal church, self, and biological families.
- Daniel mourned for three entire weeks (i.e., twenty-one days).
- Daniel abstained from tasty food (i.e., party food or desserts, meat, and wine).

This could include potato chips, candy, salted and buttered popcorn, fast foods, Starbucks, all desserts, meat (i.e., beef, chicken, or pork), wine, soda pop, and caffeinated beverages.

For those who are on medication or have health issues it may mean to fast from watching television or using the telephone (except for work, school, etc.).

If you decide to fast from food items — make sure you drink plenty of water!

Prayer Strategy:

Our main focus in calling this fast is to seek the Lord for His will, guidance, and direction, and for His protection and covering. Pray for resources. Pray for families. Pray for reconciliation. Pray for an outpouring of God's love and direction. We are asking the Lord to "Habakkuk 2:2-3": "Write down the revelation and make it plain on tablets so that a herald may run with it. For the revelation awaits an appointed time; it speaks of the end and will not prove false. Though it lingers, wait for it. It will certainly come and will not delay."

- Prepare your heart for the fast by praising and worshiping God.
- Begin with prayer to the Lord; repent of any sins.
- Establish a time each day to spend alone with God.
- Read your Bible daily.
- Be specific in your requests to God.
- Be expectant regarding answers. Consider keeping a prayer journal to record thoughts, prayers, and answers.

- Be aware of the enemy's strategies. Prepare a list of Scriptures to build up your faith during times of testing and struggle.
- Get a prayer partner, someone you can call when you need strength or feel overwhelmed, to pray for you and with you.
- When you feel temptation to eat what you have decided to give up, or watch TV, or break the fast... try praying, reading the Word, and worshiping.

Some of you may decide to take the twenty-one-day fast. Others may decide to only fast each Wednesday from 6:00 a.m. until 6:00 p,m,. And still others may decide to go for a forty-day fast. Whatever you decide, do it to the glory of God.

It's totally up to you how you will enter into this fast.

Seven Minutes: Seven (7)-minute prayer three (3) days per week.

- Each Sunday morning between the hours of 6 a.m.–8 a.m. (for seven minutes) praying for worship. *(Local church and churches across the world)*
- Each Wednesday between the hours of 6 a.m.–12 noon (for seven minutes) praying for the missions.
- Then choose another day out of the week to spend seven minutes for your family and self.

The Seven Minutes of Prayer model was designed by Dr. Kevin R. Dudley, Sr. Pastor of the The Church at North Pointe, and has been impactful in changing lives within this community.

This is totally up to you if you decide to join in this time of prayer and fasting. The Lord has impressed upon the heart of many that the Lord is calling all of us to some sort of prayer time that could include fasting as we seek the face of the Lord for "what's next" for our local churches, our communities, missional ministry, government, schools, students, marriages, sickness, pastors, world peace, being watchmen/women, and we seek to continue to do ministry.

NOTES:

_____
_____
_____
_____
_____
_____
_____
_____
_____
_____
_____
_____
_____
_____
_____
_____
_____
_____
_____
_____
_____
_____
_____
_____
_____
_____
_____
_____

X

HEARING THE VOICE OF GOD

"While Jeremiah was still confined in the courtyard
of the guard, the word of the Lord came to him
a second time: 'This is what the Lord says, he who
made the earth, the Lord who formed it and established
it—the Lord is his name: "Call to me and I will answer
you and tell you great and unsearchable things
you do not know." ' "
Jeremiah 33:1-3 NIV

Call unto God—He will answer—He will tell you
things.

God will not only hear our prayers, but He will answer
our prayers.

Our response reveals one of two things about us:

- A rebellious spirit or...
- A submissive spirit

Many of God's people spend their lives making decisions based on "their" knowledge, "their" understanding, and "their" experiences.

God wants to show us Himself (Philippians 3:7-8).

- vs. 8 "...of knowing Christ Jesus my Lord..."
  In order to hear the voice of God, I must "Know" God, not knowing about God, BUT to "Know" God, being so in tune and in touch that our heartbeat is with His.

Antithesis (The Problem):

I can't hear God – I don't know if it is God speaking – Whose voice is whose...?

John 10:3-10 NIV

"The watchman opens the gate for him, and the sheep listen to his voice. He calls his own sheep by name and leads them out. When he has brought out all of his own, he goes on ahead of them, and his sheep follow him because they know his voice. But they will never follow a stranger; in fact, they will run away from him because they do not recognize a stranger's voice." Jesus used this figure of speech, but they did not understand what he was telling them. Therefore, Jesus said again, "I tell you the truth, I am the gate for the sheep. All who ever came before me were thieves and robbers, but the sheep did not listen to them. I am the gate;

whoever enters through me will be saved. He will come in and go out, and find pasture. The thief comes only to steal and kill and destroy; I have come that they may have life, and have it to the full."

Question:

Who are you listening to? _____
_____
_____
_____
_____

Unless Statement:

Distractions:

Unless you control or get rid of the distractions in your life — they may prevent you from hearing the voice of God.

Jesus Prays for You

Living a life of hope is knowing that Jesus prays for us individually and by name. In Luke 22:31-32a, Jesus tells Peter, "Simon, Simon, Satan has asked to sift you as wheat. But I have prayed for you, Simon, that your faith may not fail."

How often in the midnight hour has the Lord called out to you by name and you awoke to say, "Yes, Lord"? As we develop that intimate relationship with Christ, day in and day out, He is always speaking. I recall times when I hear my name called to find myself in a quiet space listening and asking, "What is God speaking?" It is easy to get caught up in our day- to-day activities, walking out our fleshly desires, without checking in with the Lord. How easy it is to lose sight of the Word of the Lord and give in to doubt and unbelief, as Peter did. However, even after Peter denied Jesus three times, Peter's faith surged again when he saw Christ alive after the crucifixion. Peter went on to preach a great sermon at Pentecost, stood boldly for the Lord, and wrote letters of faith to all believers.

At times I ask myself if Jesus is praying that my faith not fail. In the book of Luke, Peter must have looked back to that word from the Lord in the dark hours after he had denied Jesus. Did Peter remember Jesus speaking, "I have prayed that you will not lose your faith"? The Lord's prayer for Peter became a life-changing reality.

What is true for Peter is true for all of God's people. "Therefore He is able to save completely those who come to God through him, because He always lives to intercede for them." (Hebrews 7:25) This tells me, "No matter what you are going through, God is there interceding on your and my behalf." What a wonderful life to live knowing that God will never leave us or forsake us.

Be encouraged! Jesus is praying for you individually.

NOTES:

_____

_____

_____

_____

_____

_____

_____

_____

_____

_____

_____

_____

_____

_____

_____

_____

_____

_____

_____

_____

_____

_____

_____

_____

XI

WORSHIP IS A LIFESTYLE

"But an hour is coming, and now is,
when the true worshipers shall worship the Father
in spirit and truth; for such people the Father seeks
to be His worshipers."
John 4:23

The reason we exist is to worship the Lord from the time we wake until the time we lay down at night. When we come together on one accord, we come to praise and worship Jesus, our Lord and our Savior. We come bringing our full selves: body, mind, spirit, soul, and heart. We give our all to Christ.

What is your reason for worship? _____

_____

_____

_____

_____

In your time of worship, do you give room for the move of the Holy Spirit? Explain. _____

_____

_____

_____

_____

_____

When we read the Book of Acts we find these words:

"When the day of Pentecost came, they were all together in one place. Suddenly a sound like the blowing of a violent wind came from heaven and filled the whole house where they were sitting. They saw what seemed to be tongues of fire that separated and came to rest on each of them. All of them were filled with the Holy Spirit and began to speak in other tongue as the Spirit enabled them." Acts 2:1-4 NIV

Does your worship bring about a wind? Explain.

_____

_____

_____

_____

_____

_____

_____

Worship is a lifestyle and your lifestyle as you worship brings Holy Spirit Power. Did you know:

- The wind displayed on the day of Pentecost is the power of the Holy Spirit?
- This power when the wind blows will never break you?
- This power—the power of the Holy Spirit—is an outpouring that God has made available to you, but it is up to you to receive it?
- This power will have you speaking another language?
- This power will have you hearing things like never before?
- This power will fill you?
- This power will move you?
- This power will change your life?

What are your thoughts about this sort of power in your life? _____

_____

_____

_____

_____

_____

When we worship God in spirit and in truth, He meets us while we worship. Read Zechariah 14:17: "If any of the people of the earth do not go up to Jerusalem to worship the King, the Lord Almighty, they will have no rain." In the words of Bishop Joseph L. Garlington, Sr., PhD, Senior Pastor of Covenant Church of Pittsburgh, a multiracial and cross-cultural community of more than two thousand members: "No Worship — No Rain!"

Do you want to see a change in your life? Worship Him. Worshiping Christ will tear down strongholds. Worshiping Christ sends God the message that you will praise and worship Him no matter the situation or circumstance. When we truly are worshiping, we place our focus on God. Worship is our faith response to Christ.

Allow me to explain "worship." First and foremost, worship is different than praise. More often than not, we confuse the two. Praise is lifting our hands and lifting our voices. Praise is giving a hallelujah. Praise is singing and dancing. I think you get the picture of praise.

List some ways you praise the Lord. _____

_____

_____

_____

_____

_____

_____

_____

_____

_____

Worship is more than lifting our hands up unto the Lord. To worship is to give our entire selves to Him sacrificially. It is literally forgetting about ourselves and giving ourselves over to Christ. It's blocking out everything around us and communing with God. As I sat through a training session, I learned that there are twelve different Hebrew and Greek words translated as "worship" in the Bible. All four Hebrew words, and especially the primary word *shachah*, mean "to depress, prostrate oneself (in homage to royalty or God) — bow down, crouch, fall down (flat), humbly beseech, do reverence, make to stoop, worship!" When we worship God, we are saying, "God, it's truly not about me; it has everything to do with You."

How often do you associate food, clothing, an event, material things, etc., to the word, "awesome?"

_____

_____

_____

_____

_____

_____

_____

We misuse the word, "awesome." I, too, have to catch myself at times. I immediately will say when I truly like something, "That's awesome." What??? Only God is awesome, so why do I try and place things in the same category or on the same level as Christ? That's wrong. There is none like Him – no, not one or not one thing! We use the word "awesome" in everyday life. We use it to describe people at times. No! Only God is "Awesome!" He is higher than anyone else. He is more powerful. He is amazing. He is King. He is Lord of lords and high and lifted up. He is the only One worthy of honor. His awesomeness is what moves us to worship Him.

How will you change using the word "awesome?"

_____

_____

_____

_____

_____

_____

When you worship, you give your full self. You are submitting everything to Him. During worship there's a sweet...I really cannot explain it – He is that awesome. He leaves me speechless. It's having a melody in your spirit and it's unexplainable. It's pure surrender. "I have my face and my body bowed before the Lord. I have tears rolling down my face." The presence of the Lord is here. Can't you sense His presence? Now that's worship. There's a stillness and a quiet spirit. You are in a space of not being able to move. There's a hush groaning in your belly but still no words. Worship Him. Worship Christ!

It is a time in worship that the enemy cannot penetrate this moment with the Lord as you worship Christ. Nothing else matters but Jesus. Worship Him! It is thinking, "I want to stay here. I don't want anyone or anything to disturb this time with me and God."

Can you remember the last time you truly worshiped Christ? Write it here. Give details.

_____

_____

_____

_____

_____

_____

_____

_____

_____

_____

_____

_____

_____

_____

_____

_____

_____

_____

_____

_____

Now what are you going to do to find your way back into that space of truly worshiping Christ? _____

_____

_____

_____

_____

_____

_____

_____

_____

_____

_____

_____

_____

_____

_____

_____

_____

_____

_____

_____

_____

_____

_____

_____

_____

Let us pray.

Father God, we worship You in spirit and in truth. You are God. You are Awesome. You are Amazing. We surrender ourselves completely to You, Lord; I desire to rest in Your arms. I want my heartbeat to beat with Yours. I am Yours. I surrender everything to You. I am nothing without You. Speak peace to my spirit. In Jesus' name, AMEN.

NOTES:

XII

COME AWAY

Reading the book of Luke is eye-opening. We find that many times after Jesus has performed miracles, gathered with others, or made decisions as in appointing His disciples, "He often withdrew to the wilderness to pray." (Luke 5:16 TLB)

WOW! Jesus knew to withdraw to the wilderness to pray after He had ministered in His way to others.

Could it be that we become weary because we have not taken the time to withdraw and pray? Explain your answer. _____

_____

_____

_____

_____

_____

_____

_____

After all you have done personally in any given day to glorify the Lord, do you withdraw to pray? Explain your answer. _____

_____

_____

_____

_____

_____

_____

_____

_____

Do you think there would be a difference in your every-day life if you did withdraw to pray after you have ministered to another person? Explain. _____

_____

_____

_____

_____

_____

_____

You can find many Scriptures in Luke that will reveal the times Jesus "went away to pray." In my daily reading, here are a few Scriptures that spoke clearly to my spirit.

Luke 5:16
Luke 6:12-13
Luke 9:10

Please reread each Scripture and write out your thoughts. How can you apply these Scriptures to your prayer life?

_____

_____

_____

_____

_____

_____

_____

_____

_____

_____

_____

_____

_____

It is important, as we minister the Gospel of Jesus Christ to others, to "Come Away" and spend some quiet time with God. We find this in the Bible in Jeremiah 33:3, when God says, "Call to me and I will answer you and tell you great and unsearchable things you do not know." This is in our intimate time with the Lord that we call out to Him.

How do you "Come Away?" Please explain. _____

_____

_____

_____

_____

Prior to ministering to an individual or to groups of people, I have learned to seek God and ask Him, "Lord, what do You want?" just as Jesus did prior to appointing His twelve disciples. In Luke 6:12-13, it reads, "One day soon afterwards he went out into the mountains to pray, and prayed all night. At daybreak he called together his followers and chose twelve of them to be the inner circle of his disciples." It's when we have important decisions to make or ministry to administer that we must "Come Away" with Jesus to seek His will in the situation. After we pray and seek His will, we are able to minister to His children and to individuals seeking Him. And then, after the ministering, we return to Him to be refueled.

Do you ask God, "What are you speaking?" before you pray? If not, what can you do to ask the question and hear from God prior to praying? If you do, explain.

_____

_____

_____

_____

The enemy comes to steal, kill, and destroy, BUT Jesus came to bring life and life in abundance. (John 10:10) May I encourage you to seek Christ first—spend time with Him in prayer prior to your ministering to others. Ask, "God, what are You speaking?" "What do You desire?" Then after you have ministered, return to God and be filled with His holy power.

"Ready to Pray" means one must go deeper in the Word of the Lord. As we get better acquainted with the Word of God, the Bible, we grow to know God better and gain wisdom and revelation knowledge to pray in accordance with His will.

How do you plan to go deeper with Christ? _____

_____

_____

_____

_____

_____

_____

_____

_____

_____

_____

_____

_____

_____

_____

NOTES:

XIII

SPEAK LIFE

"The tongue has the power of life and death,
and those who love it will eat its fruit."
Proverbs 18:21

The power of words! We have the power to speak
life or death. What a responsibility! What are we
speaking?

Imagine driving with teenagers and you enter into a
discussion about boys and how some of the girls in high
school dress inappropriately. Imagine the conversation
going something like this, "Libby came to school today
wearing six-inch heels and a skirt that showed her 'boy
shorts.' I did not think she showed respect to herself—
let alone anyone else. What do you think?" Or you enter
into a conversation that begins, "How do you deal with
individuals who are without Christ?" Usually there is
a bit of silence. Therefore, one must inquire of the Lord

how exactly to answer or if you are to answer. This is when we say, "Speak life." How should we "speak life?"

This is a question for all of us. How should we speak life? Think about the times you have spoken words that possibly destroyed another. It was not your intention to do so, but the words you spoke caused a type of death in the life of another. How often we speak words that create an environment that makes one feel less than they truly are. One word could either give life or give death. As I write out this devotional, I wonder to myself, "How many people have I killed with the power of my tongue?" Ouch!

If the power of life and death is in the tongue — and if God's words are life and healing — then it seems to follow that we should make every effort to speak God's Word over our lives and the lives of everyone around us.

In this season, so much is happening. As you go through any sort of transition, are you speaking life or death? Are we sharing the Good News or the bad news? Are we sharing the hopes and dreams or merely our negative perception? We have been given authority to speak life and to speak those things which are not as though they were. Why then, do we continue to talk about our problems instead of speaking life?

Speak by His Spirit. Speak life to grow your ministry. Speak life in your church and church family. Speak life into Bible studies. Speak restoration into the relationships of the people around you that may be experiencing difficulty. Speak reconciliation to marriages of your neighbors, family members, coworkers, and so on. Speak the mending of your broken heart. Speak peace into chaos. Speak life into dry bones. Speak unity into your family. We have the authority to do all that. Speak it AND believe it.

Our thoughts determine our feelings and our feelings determine our actions. Actions will become habits. Whatever you keep your mind on is what you will manifest in your life. If things aren't going well, think about them being correct. Instead of focusing on the problem, capture the solution.

Remember that our God is a God of *life*. When Jesus hung on the cross, all of our "stuff" hung there with Him. When He died, our "stuff" died. When He arose, we were resurrected too, and there was life. (See Ephesians 1:17-23 and 2:1-10.)

Let's stop speaking death. We must speak life!

What areas in your life do you believe you need to speak life? _____

_____

_____

_____

_____

_____

_____

_____

Can you identify any conversations where you spoke death? List the names of the individuals who you shared things which were not life-speaking: _____

_____

_____

_____

_____

_____

_____

_____

_____

_____

_____

Now write a prayer to speak life into the lives of the individuals you may have spoken death: _____

_____

_____

_____

_____

_____

_____

_____

_____

_____

_____

_____

Speaking life to yourself and to others around you would help your prayer life in what way? _____

_____

_____

_____

_____

_____

_____

_____

_____

Thinking back over your life, can you identify any time where someone may have spoken into your life? What was the spoken word, life or death? If it was a word of death, how did you or will you overcome in that area? Write out a prayer here that turns that spoken word around.

_____

_____

_____

_____

_____

_____

_____

_____

_____

_____

NOTES:

XIV

Pray and Faint Not

"Walk and Pray," also known as "Prayer-walking," is simply praying as you are walking. It's walking around your neighborhood, the community, or from your car in a parking lot, with a purpose. Passing by homes, families outside playing, gardening, watering the lawn? Pray God's anointing. Passing by cars? Pray God's protection so they may not run into or be a part of an accident. Walking through the local government offices, school, or work location? Why not lift up a prayer of divine intervention? Cover these areas with God's presence as you walk. Yes, it's multitasking, but with a purpose; a divine assignment calling forth God's ministering angels and the Lord's mighty presence.

Thesis:

By intentionally becoming aware and being intentional in your prayer life, one is able to pray God-focused prayers for marriages, the lost, jobs, relationships, sale of a home, reconciliation, churches, church leadership, pastors, safety, youth, young children, single moms and single dads, deliverance of a stronghold, domestic situations, illnesses, healing, educational system, accidents, protection, and salvation. Many of these are situations that you may never have thought about if you'd been sitting at home going about your day doing whatever comes naturally. It's an opportunity to cover an entire area in prayer. It's an opportunity for God to speak to you so you may call on those things and turn them over to Jesus. "Praying and Faint Not" as you canvas an area, allows you the opportunity to get in touch with God in a powerful way. It brings about compassion and commitment between you and your neighbors, between you and the places your frequently shop or attend in and around your neighborhood/community and beyond those areas. It helps you build relationships and allows you to seek God's face for wisdom in how to respond. This is called "having a spirit of discernment."

List your frequent locations for shopping. List the schools in your local community, and list neighbors that come to mind. _____

_____

_____

_____

_____

_____

_____

To walk and pray is to be intentional in praying the authority of Jesus Christ and shows an act of confidence in God's power over particular situations. For those unable to walk, it is still intentional prayer. It is covering in prayer every place you appear. It is action — action that demonstrates a commitment to intentionally cover territory in prayer that the enemy has tried to take control. When we think about "walking," we think about moving forward in victory. Any sort of movement illustrates your belief and trust in Christ. It's lining your prayers up with the desires of God's heart and experiencing and living with hope and belief, and it is seeing the fruit of all you have prayed and petitioned for in a particular community, center, governmental office, and corporate environments. It is a statement that one declares and decrees that it belongs to Christ. This can become a movement which will stretch your faith.

What is God speaking to you about covering territory in prayer? Explain. _____

_____

_____

_____

_____

_____

_____

_____

_____

If God leads you to build a team to cover territory in prayer, we would encourage several small groups within a neighborhood, workplace, or organization, to host "Bible Studies." Why not start with this book, your "Ready to Pray" workbook?

Antithesis:

- Do not be deceived. Cover territory with prayer and seek the face of the Lord. Pray "Thy will be done." If you cover territory through "Prayer-walking," please do not consider this a time of losing those unwanted pounds. It does, however, become a benefit but not the focus. Be careful that when covering territory, it does not distract you from Jesus. This is not a time to gain the latest gossip and this is not a "Social Club" you are join-ing. The enemy will try to "steal, kill, and destroy. However, Jesus came to bring life and to bring in life more abundantly."
- Be mindful of "spiritual warfare." Covering terri-tory in prayer opens you to receive all that the Holy Spirit is showing you. Your level of discernment increases and you become sensitive of the environ-ment. Warfare will come, especially while praying for restoration and the lost. This will require per-sistence and patience.

Unless:

Unless we cover our neighborhoods in prayer the enemy will sneak in and try to gain a foothold to destroy households, schools, neighborhoods, marriages, children, leadership, and possibly churches.

Why cover territory through prayer? _____
_____
_____
_____
_____
_____
_____

Synthesis:

1. Cover neighborhoods for Christ through intentional prayer.
2. Display victory in Jesus Christ.
3. Make disciples.
4. Show true dependence on God.
5. Watch God move.

Implement:

1. *Seek God.*

   Remove yourself and your personal desires. Pray God's heart. Ask, "God, what are you speaking?"

2. *Begin with praise and worship and lift up any concerns of the territory you are covering in prayer.*

   Consecrate yourself to God. Study the Word of God. Identify Scriptures to cover territory in prayer. Focus your attention on what you are about to do and remind yourself why you are doing it. Be quiet before God for a while and listen to Him just before you go out in order to tune yourself in to His voice. Be Holy Spirit-led.

3. *Build relationships within the team if you are not doing this alone.*

   Make sure everyone in your team gets to know each other before you begin, so that you are all familiar and comfortable with each other. Most importantly, make sure effective prayer is not being compromised by disagreements or religious talks that may cause a division between members of the team.

4. *Organize the walk (if you are doing this as a walk).*
   NOTE: This may be adjusted for however you are covering territory in prayer.

   Divide into groups of two or three, so there are enough in a group to support each other (remember that prayer is sealed by agreement). Make sure that confident or experienced intercessors are split up between the groups. Determine the route for action. Be sure to cover all the areas that you feel need prayer, for whatever reason. Different groups can walk in different directions and may take longer over certain parts than others. Determine how long you are going to spend. Make sure that all the groups know when they should return but be flexible in the timing. Thirty minutes to an hour is usually the recommendation to begin.

   a. What specifically are you praying about? Pray for God's presence in a particular area. Encourage people to bring a small Bible to pray Scriptures and read out passages they feel are relevant to a particular situation.

   Most importantly, make sure that you take time to define the purpose of the prayer walk beforehand. What is it you want God to achieve in that place?

List your perspective team: _____

_____

_____

_____

_____

_____

_____

You must identify a strong team leader for each neighborhood.

Have the team leader sign up online at www. ReadytoPray.info under "Pray and Faint Not."

NOTES:

_____

_____

_____

_____

_____

_____

_____

_____

_____

_____

_____

_____

_____

_____

_____

_____

_____

_____

_____

_____

_____

_____

_____

_____

_____

_____

_____

XV

EXPERIENCE THE MIRACULOUS

"So Peter was kept in prison, but the church was
earnestly praying to God for him."
Acts 12:5 NIV

Have you ever been in a situation that the only way
to get out of it was to go through it? Explain.

_____

_____

_____

_____

_____

_____

_____

_____

Take Peter. In Acts 12, Peter was seized by King Herod
during the Feast of Unleavened Bread. Peter was placed

in jail and handed over to four soldiers. There were plans to have Peter brought before the public after the Passover. Peter was in a bad situation, but the church was praying.

Have you been in such a challenging situation where others began to pray? If so, explain. _____

_____

_____

_____

_____

_____

_____

_____

_____

Read Acts 12:1-19. What are your thoughts about the miracle upon Peter? _____

_____

_____

_____

_____

_____

_____

_____

_____

_____

Have you personally experienced the miraculous? Please
explain. _____

_____

_____

_____

_____

_____

_____

What Is a Miracle?

It is an amazing event, which triggers one to be in awe.
A miracle may be described in the following ways:

- An unexplainable extraordinary event.
- An incident, which causes individuals to witness a
  phenomenal experience.
- A supernatural intervention that comes unexpect-
  edly, but right on time.
- Immeasurable — an unexplainable act.
- God's divine covering and protection when you
  cannot see your way out of a situation.
- An unexpected answer when you have not shared
  it with anyone but God.
- A divine appointment that cannot be explained.
- The manifestation of God's presence and awe-
  inspiring love.

- An awestruck moment. An experience that you would not believe if you weren't a part of the experience.

Miracles are not solely works of possibility or familiar answers to prayer. Miracles as defined in the dictionary are, "An event that cannot be explained by the known laws of nature and is therefore attributed to divine intervention." Miracles as displayed in the Bible are:

- Elijah praying for fire on the altar (1 Kings 18:23, 24)
- The woman with the issue of bleeding (Mark 5:21-34)
- Jairus' twelve-year-old daughter (Mark 5:36-42)
- The woman bent for eighteen years (Luke 13:10-13)
- Lazarus (John 11:38-44)
- The lame man of thirty-eight years (John 5:1-9)

And we also have...

- Calming of the sea (Matthew 8:23-27)
- The blind men healed (Matthew 9:27-31)
- A man with the withered hand (Matthew 12:10-14)
- The feeding of the multitude (Matthew 14:13-21)
- Jesus walking on water (Matthew 14:22-32)
- Cursing of the fig tree (Matthew 21:18-22)
- Casting the net to catch many fish (Luke 5:1-11)

- The prison doors opened after praying and singing hymns (Acts 16:25-26)

Then there were the miracles of the disciples throughout the Book of Acts chapters 9, 13, and 19, 1 Corinthians 12, Galatians 3, and also in Hebrews 2.

List other Scriptures where you see miracles in the Bible.

_____

_____

_____

_____

_____

_____

Never confuse the miracles of God as a work of magic. Works of magic are not of God. Miracles of God performed by the hands of God should be characterized as works of God, not of magic.

How Can We Expect the Miraculous?

Miracles, such as the healing of the woman who was bleeding for twelve years, come by faith. She had faith enough to take a risk and touch the hem of Jesus' garment. She had faith to believe that if she could simply touch the hem, she would be made well. She did not have a formula and she did not perform some sort of ritual. She simply had a little faith. Jesus said, if you have faith even as small as a mustard seed, you can tell your mountain (obstacle, hindrance, or problem) to move and nothing will be impossible for you. (Matthew 17:20) — *as long as it lines up with the will of the Lord.*

How much faith do you have when praying for the miraculous for yourself or for someone else? Please explain.

_____

_____

_____

_____

_____

How Shall I Pray?

If praying for the miraculous or praying to intercede on behalf on another we must...

- Look to God, the author and the finisher of our faith, asking Him to have His way. Seek God regarding the situation. Pray and say to God, "Thy will be done."
- Ask God what He is speaking.
- Once you ask, wait on Jesus to respond. Ask God to give you revelation knowledge.
- Study the Word of the Lord both day and night. Pray and seek God's will through reading His Word.
- Believe God.

- Experiencing the miraculous is not manipulating God.

How will you pray when a miracle is needed? _____

_____

_____

_____

_____

_____

_____

_____

_____

_____

NOTES:

XVI

PRAYER POSITIONS

Each of these positions (and others) can be done for any kind of praying, but each has special meaning for different kinds of prayer. Standing with hands raised is typical of praise, celebrative prayer, and thanksgiving. Kneeling and prostration show humility and recognition of a superior, and thus are especially well-suited to prayers of confession, repentance, or awe. (If you're someone who bows to no one, consider praying while lying prostrate in public with everyone watching.) Slow wandering is especially good for meditational prayer and for quieting yourself so you can listen. Standing while facing the altar with other people who are also worshiping is part of an act of worship. Other positions have been used as well. For example, Elijah crouched low to the ground and put his face between his knees. The Bible does not mention arm gestures in prayer except the raising of hands. Christians praying together are known to link hands and raise them together. These positions can help you pray right, by getting your body into (or, sometimes, out of the way of) your prayers, and as a way to express what the prayer is for. Prayer is done with your whole self, and the body is part of that. The key is that you are having a living response with God, speaking and listening. Whatever position your body is in, God is still paying attention, and the leading of the Holy Spirit as you yield to Him is more important than the position you are in. The openness of your heart is ultimately what counts.

kneeling

bowing

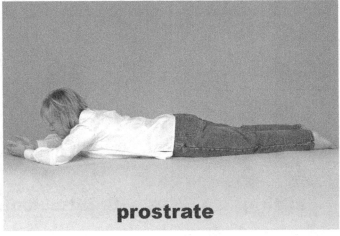

prostrate

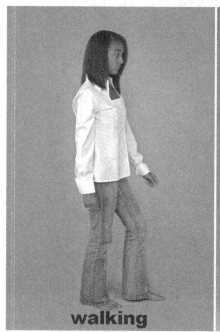

walking

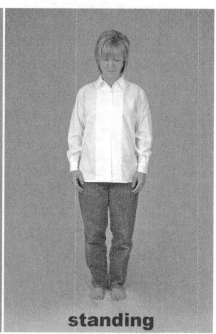

standing

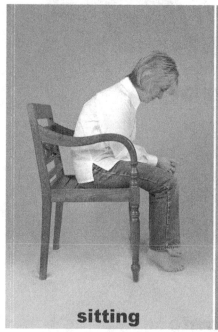

sitting

with lifted hands

† **Kneeling,** head bowed, hands folded (1 Kings 8:54; Ezra 9:5; Luke 22:41; Acts 9:40)

† **Bowing,** head to the ground, hands face down on the ground next to head (Exodus 34:8; Nehemiah 8:6; Psalm 72:11)

† **Laying flat,** on the floor, face down, with hands stretched out *(prostrate)* (Joshua 7:6; Ezra 10:1; Matthew 26:39; Mark 14:35)

† **Slow, leisurely walking,** eyes open *(walking)* (2 Kings 4:35)

† **Standing,** head slightly bowed, facing the altar (Nehemiah 9:5; Mark 11:25; Luke 18:13)

† **Sitting,** head bowed, leaning forward, eyes closed, hands folded (1 Chronicles 17:16-27)

† **With lifted hands,** hands raised and spread, palms up, eyes looking upward (2 Chronicles 6:12, 13; Psalm 63:4; 1 Timothy 2:8)

NOTES:

_____

_____

_____

_____

_____

_____

_____

_____

_____

_____

_____

_____

_____

_____

_____

_____

_____

_____

_____

_____

_____

_____

_____

_____

_____

XVII

URGENT PLEA FOR PRAYER

Gathering the community in prayer brings about unity and a force to collectively seek the throne of God on behalf of others. The purpose of our prayer meeting was to pray for children, teens, and young adults across the nations. Additionally, this call to an urgent plea for prayer is to encourage prayer teams to continue in ongoing prayer within their communities, schools, corporations, hospitals, and churches.

The "Urgent Plea for Prayer" initiative began in the fall of 2009. This effort was so important because it brought people together from across the nations and all denominations to pray for young people. It was set to take place on December 12, 2009, for twelve hours. In the end, we lifted by name over twenty-two thousand people unto the Lord.

Stephanie Bright Mayberry, one of the intercessors during this plea for prayer, stated, "Looking at the needs and prayer requests for these children is looking at the very same issues we have as adults. If someone would have taken the time to pray for us as children, maybe we wouldn't be in these situations today." Another intercessor, Patricia Lyles, who is employed at a children's hospital, shared, "As we prayed over the children in the hospital beds, we realized that we needed to pray for the parents of these children as well."

This is a beginning of an ongoing prayer movement to pray for children, teens, and young adults across the nations.

You are reading a real-life prayer movement which can serve as an example for you and your teams as you implement a prayer gathering.

Thesis:

When you join in intercession one with another, breakthroughs happen, people are delivered, healing takes place, lives are changed, and the power of the Lord is upon you.

Sharing prayer requests is a form of confession. We find in James 5:16: "Confess your faults one to another, and pray one for another, that ye may be healed. The effectual fervent prayer of a righteous man availeth much."

Antithesis:

"But I do not have time to pray. There's so much going on in my busy life, I don't have time to intercede on behalf of another."

Isaiah 62:6a: "I have posted watchmen on your walls, O Jerusalem; they will never be silent day or night."

Colossians 4:2: "Devote yourselves to prayer, being watchful and thankful."

Unless:

Unless we watch and pray on behalf of another, people will remain in bondage, people will live defeated lives, people will be trapped by the enemy, people will walk around confused, people will give up.

Question:

What happens when we join together in prayer over a period of time, praying collectively over one area?

_____

_____

_____

_____

_____

_____

Synthesis:

People from around the world come together on the same day at the same time (no matter the time zone) to pray. The impact is great. On December 12, 2009, many intercessors came together for twelve hours (7 a.m.–7 p.m.) to pray for children, teens, and young adults. We lifted by name over twenty-two thousand individuals. Individual people, teams, and congregations joined in prayer in the United States; Ghana; New Zealand; Uganda; Johannesburg, South Africa; Kenya; Durban; Papua, New Guinea; Australia; and Nigeria. Before the twelve hours were completed, praise reports began to be reported.

Implementation:

- Pray and ask God for direction.
- Get a team of volunteers to serve in the roles of administration, intercessors, hosting locations, etc.
- Determine the date for the prayer gathering.
- Determine the reason for praying "For this reason I bow…, Ephesians 3:14."
- Determine the timeframe for intercession.
- Ask for team coordinators to coordinate a team in each community, state, country, etc.
- Have a system in place in order to keep track of all prayer requests, e-mails, and team coordinators.
- Organize the marketing efforts.

- Send out an announcement of the prayer gathering.
- Fast and pray.

Urgent Plea for Prayer is to seek the face and heart of God on behalf of the call for prayer. It is not a time to seek His hand or His blessing. The desire is meet Him and to intercede or stand in the gap expressing the need for His grace to be bestowed upon others.

Prayer Models:

There are arrays of ways of coming together to pray on behalf of others during a prayer gathering that will help maintain the enthusiasm of those who are participating. Listed below are four models of prayer which you might like to introduce to your team for possible prayer gatherings.

1. **Small Groups**

   The team leader of each prayer gathering brings together a team to pray over the cause/need. Each team leader would send out an announcement to invite the community, neighborhood, or subdivision for a time of prayer. The announcement could read something like this: "We invite you to join our time of prayer on (date). Would you please consider joining our group to pray during this prayer gathering?"

Include additional information such as the location and time. You may also include suggested materials or requests for prayer as well. Materials could include: water, Bible, pen, paper, journal, etc.

The team leader determines the outline for the time of prayer. The team leader may decide to have five, seven, or twelve intercessors, each to pray for one hour; or you may decide to have the entire team pray collectively for three, seven, twelve, or twenty-four hours, etc.

2. **Acts 4**

This may be in a church setting or a house setting or in a park, etc. Acts 4 involves everyone praying aloud at the same time. This is found in Acts 4:24. The leader, having introduced the cause/need to be prayed, will direct those present to pray in this way. Some people may decide to pray silently during this time of prayer. That is not a problem. The purpose is to have everyone praying.

3. **Walk and Pray**

You may decide to have a team of individuals walking and praying during the prayer gathering. The team leader will share the prayer requests of the community where the team will walk and pray. The group may decide to walk and pray together or split up and take different areas of the community to ensure that every area is covered in prayer.

4. Silent Prayer

As a contrast to the above models, silence can be very effective at a prayer gathering. One may find the need to sit and read Scriptures during the time of prayer, inserting names of individuals throughout the Scriptures in place of the words "Me" and "You."

Selecting clear and confident team leaders is important. Most people feel reassured, relax, and pray more effectively with strong leadership and a strong foundation. It may help to have more than one team leader involved. Ready to Pray Ministries will provide pens and pads for people to write down any prophetic words, impressions, or Bible verses, if interested.

Checklist:

1. Six to Seven Months before the "Urgent Plea for Prayer"

a. Select a suitable venue.

b. If this is a workshop: Reserve a laptop, projector, or overhead projector (OHP) and screen for the venue and ensure that you have a projectionist/overhead operator.

c. Recruit a technical coordinator who will plan and oversee lights, sounds, projection, music, etc., for the prayer conference or gathering.

   d. Invite a worship leader and praise team during the worship time or use CDs .

   e. If using "Live Stream," check that the venue has microphones, extension leads, and enough electrical sockets and computer internet services.

   f. Make sure that OHP acetates/projection slides are available for the songs that are to be used.

2. The Day of the "Urgent Plea for Prayer"

   a. Put up signs directing people to the venue.

   b. Arrive early to prepare and for individuals who may come earlier than the meeting time.

   c. Check that the projector/OHP and screen are in place and ready to go.

   d. Have bottled water for each participant.

   e. Check that pens and paper are available.

You may decide to have some sort of fellowship at the end of the conference or prayer gathering so that people can have a chance to meet others from different ministries and churches or to discuss ideas and other events.

What Next?

Make sure that individuals and groups turn in praise reports so that others get the reports of answered prayer.

Sample Letters

Letter to church leaders and community leaders:

Dear [name],

Re: Prayer for [your area]
We would love to invite you and members of your church/community to our upcoming prayer gathering (or conference). This gathering will take place on (DATE) from (time) to (time).

This involves prayer for (insert the cause/need to be prayed for).

This is a wonderful opportunity for [insert your area] churches to come together to pray for the cause/need and the transformation of our community.

We have enclosed information on this gathering/conference. May I encourage you to hand out the enclosed flyers to your congregation/community?

We understand that there will be hundreds of similar prayer meetings taking place up and down the country throughout the year. It is exciting to be part of a nationwide prayer initiative and I hope that you will be able to join us.

In Obedience to Christ,

Letter to intercessors

Beloved:

Re: Prayer for [your area]

Same as indicated in the letter above but add the following:

We would love for you to lead a team in your area. If you feel the Lord is calling you to this time of prayer, please reply to our letter by calling (telephone) or e-mailing us at (e-mail address). We look forward to joining you in prayer on behalf of children, teens, and young adults across the nations.

For more information, ideas and training:

Have you or your team ever attended a "Ready to Pray" Workshop or gathering? It is a one-day/5-hour Journey of Prayer instruction designed to equip individuals, groups, and churches that desire to go deeper in their prayer journey and who want effective and impactful prayer gatherings. For details of future conferences, please visit the website www.ReadytoPray.info.

Would you like assistance on hosting a "5-Hour Journey of Prayer Instruction" conference or prayer gathering? Ministry in Motion Ministries is available to assist you. MIMToday will sow 10 percent of any profit into your ministry or church. The cost per person for the conference is $50.00 (non-refundable) and includes the *Ready To Pray Workbook*. Lunch is not included but can be arranged between the host and participants.

MIMToday will supply the postcards for promotions and will prepare the Constant Contact announcement sent to the host to forward through their e-mail distribution list. For more information, contact Gail Dudley at GED@MIMToday.org or call 614-441-8178 for more information.

NOTES:

_____

_____

_____

_____

_____

_____

_____

_____

_____

_____

_____

_____

_____

_____

_____

_____

_____

_____

_____

_____

_____

_____

_____

_____

_____

_____

_____

XVIII

24-Hour Prayer Gathering

Scripture Reference:

- "For This Cause I Bow...." Ephesians 3:14 KJV

Mission:

Unite believers of Christ in an ongoing dynamic journey of prayer.

Purpose:

A "Prayer Gathering" will lead attendees through understanding the essential elements of prayer and its need in today's society for an appointed time. Believers are encouraged to come expecting a "Life-Strengthening, Life-Transforming" time with the Lord.

This is a time of extended prayer and worship experience, and a time of listening and seeking the Lord on behalf of others (community, government, leadership, families, etc.). This is a time of coming together with other believers seeking God with the hope that He will reveal great and mighty things we know not. (Jeremiah 33:3)

Focus:

The focus is on personal and community transformation that results in experiencing life- changing reality. It is transforming mindsets which will breathe restoration, healing, deliverance, and the life-altering victory of Jesus.

This is a time for sanctification. God calls us to humble ourselves, therefore, during the twenty-four hours of set-aside time for a humbling experience which invites us to submission, brokenness, and real-life change, moving us to another level in Christ and unity among believers.

Outcome:

- Experiencing the presence of God, collectively

Sample Format:

- Begin Friday evening at 7:00 p.m. with a preached/taught word on prayer. For example, Ephesians 3:14: "For this cause I bow...." (Whatever the cause—one bows before the Father.)
- After the preached/taught word on prayer, lead the believers into collective and individual prayer.

- Each hour or so, bring the people together and ask, "What is God speaking?" Repeat this throughout the twenty-four hours.
- After hearing the spoken Word of the Lord, move again into prayer, praying what has been spoken. Repeat this throughout the twenty-four hours.
- Be flexible and have a time of quiet confession and one-on-one prayer with prayer leaders.
- At the end of the twenty-four hours, bring everyone together for a circle of prayer. Have each person speak one word (expressing thanks, presenting bodies as a living sacrifice, holy and acceptable unto Christ).
- The host will "Seal" the prayer. "Seal" means to secure a closing of the time together in prayer and to authenticate all that has been presented to the Lord. It is a prayer of protection, of closure, and of saying, "It is so in Jesus' name."

Together we can and we will embark on one of the greatest times and moments in prayer as we intercede for our cities, families, relationships, careers, pastors, churches, ministries, those who need healing, deliverance, youth, schools, government, and much more. Encourage believers to come and unit for a powerful time with the Lord.

Prior to the "Prayer Gathering":

- 7 months prior
  - o Begin meeting with partners (churches, prayer intercessors, etc.) to discuss place, date, time, etc.
  - o Ask for the partners to begin listening specifically for what "God is speaking."
- 3 months prior
  - o Begin to announce this prayer gathering.
- 2 months prior
  - o Begin receiving prayer requests.
- 1 month prior
  - o Assign individuals or teams to cover each other (be present together on site of the gathering).
- 1 week prior
  - o Remind individuals and teams of believers of the prayer gathering and begin to fast and pray.
- 1 day before
  - o Rest in the Lord.

Tools:

1. Bible
2. Journal
3. Prayer Requests

4. Posted Flip Chart paper and markers—use these to post requests throughout the twenty-four hours as people are led. Some labels for the flip chart paper: Salvation, Marriages, Special Prayers, Youth, Pastors, Government Officials, Healing, Deliverance, Restoration, Protection, and Financial Needs. NOTE: One may write names or initials of individuals, churches, etc., under each label. Be sure to include youth within the prayer gathering.

5. Bottled Water

What is your reason to host a prayer gathering? _____

_____

_____

_____

_____

_____

_____

_____

_____

Where would you host a prayer gathering? _____

_____

_____

_____

_____

_____

_____

What do you need to host a prayer gathering? _____

_____

_____

_____

_____

_____

Who would you partner with? _____

_____

_____

_____

_____

_____

What are the immediate needs for a prayer gathering?

_____

_____

_____

_____

_____

What is God speaking? _____

_____

_____

_____

_____

_____

_____

_____

_____

_____

NOTES:

_____

_____

_____

_____

_____

_____

_____

_____

_____

_____

_____

_____

_____

_____

_____

_____

_____

_____

_____

_____

_____

_____

_____

_____

_____

_____

_____

TESTIMONIALS

Gail is a woman after God's own heart. Her life is centered around the Word of God and she inspires, motivates, and mentors other women to center their life around Jesus Christ and to grow in their faith. Her energy, enthusiasm, humor, and example truly have inspired me to live for Christ with the same zeal.

— Peg Buehlman,
VP of The Rock Environmental Center, Inc.,
Ellicott City, MD

I was recently enrolled in a PhD program and I e-mailed Pastor Gail Dudley, on several occasions, requesting prayer from Ministry in Motion. I had a seemingly impossible deadline to meet and I did not see how I could complete the required tasks. The Ministry in Motion prayer warriors, like the saints in Acts 12:5 united together and prayed on my behalf. Through God's grace, I was able to complete all the requirements in a timely fashion and I graduated. The successful completion of my program is a testament of the awesome power of prayer. I am truly grateful to all the saints in Ministry in Motion for continually lifting me up in prayer.

— Franslee Thomany, Ph.D.

Prayer changes everything; seeing people's lives changed right before your eyes is a miraculous experience. The prayer summit was so powerful that some could not sleep; they had to come back because the call to pray was so strong. Pastor Gail's prayer workshops have helped me draw closer to the Lord and to become a devoted intercessor.

— Mary Owens

Gail Dudley is what I call real and authentic. She doesn't try to be something she is not. She is transparent, allowing others to come to know and understand that we all have struggles — even Christians, and even ministers of the Gospel — but through the power of the Holy Spirit we can overcome. She is not caught up in trying to please people; she seeks only to please God. Gail is a life coach and an encourager, approachable and genuine. She not only ministers the Word of God, but she also provides the tools for life applications. Last but certainly not least, she sees your potential and challenges you to walk in it.

— Kelly Shaw

Coming to the table experiencing God through studying His Word has opened my eyes. Gail gets us to step out of our comfort zone, which is growth. She is real and puts the information so that we can understand. Gail is passionate. One grows closer to Christ through her teaching.

— Tanya Palmer

For This Cause I Pray

Mary Owens shares…

Prayer is my direct line to the Father. When I can't talk to anyone else I can talk to Him. Prayer is my way of communicating with my heavenly Father. Prayer is sitting in a quite place with only you and Him, pouring out your heart, and seeing the results of your prayers being answered. I love to see prayers answered. The Bible tells us He is an on time God.

As a child my mother always made me open family devotions with prayer. What I did not know was God was preparing me for a future calling as an intercessor. Praying for others is a blessing. Watching God work in people's lives is a joy for me. I continue to pray because I am in love with God. Praying for others is my calling, and hearing from God is better than talking to Him. As I look back, it all started with prayer at night before I went to bed as a child, saying my blessing before we ate, graduating from a child's prayer to the Lord's Prayer, to asking just for myself, to now interceding for others.

— *Mary Owens,* Ohio

From Elizabeth Aouad…

WHY PRAY?

I don't remember the exact moment I began to pray. I just knew God knew my thoughts, so I began thinking toward Him. Even when I went my own way, every time I hit a point of true desperation, I cried out to God for help. As I felt Him drawing me to Him as an adult, I began to ask Him to reveal Himself to me if He was really God. He answered. I kept up the dialogue. Then, I received Christ as Savior. I fell in love. Then I hit a crisis. I fell on my face. He poured out His peace in me. He threw out holy baits. I bit. I was hooked. He *over*filled me with His Spirit. It poured out of me in a new prayer language. He called me deeper, in over my head in prayer. He asked me to believe in Him; I did. He proved faithful. He called me into the Word. I discovered His promises to me. I prayed to see them in my life. He revealed Himself in greater ways through the answers. I awake and pray or wake up praying. God is there to meet me every morning. Sometimes I cling to Him just to meet the hard challenge of another day. Why pray? Why breathe? I exhale, God inhales. God exhales, I inhale. Spirit of life, Holy Father, LORD Jesus…a trinity of love, power, and intimacy. Just a slice of why I pray!

– Elizabeth Aouad,
Author of Stand Up and Fight Like a Woman
~ A Women's Study on Spiritual Warfare

From Mary Hamrick…

Prayer is a mystery to me. It always has been and I imagine it always will be. But the one thing I understand about prayer is that it is communication with God, spirit to Spirit. Recently, I attended a prayer workshop conducted by Gail Dudley where she was demonstrating the different prayer poses and the biblical examples of how, when, and who used those specific poses. After teaching, Gail asked us to choose a prayer pose and then to get into that pose as we talked to God. What a humbling experience, to be in a roomful of women, all kneeling and praying to God. There is power in kneeling to pray before God. Gail not only taught of that power; she also allowed every woman in the workshop to experience that power through her teaching and leading. The prayer ministry that God has called Gail into is one that is proven, tested, and anointed. God speaks with authority and conviction through Gail Dudley, for she is His chosen vessel.

— *Mary Hamrick, Dragonfly Ministries,*
www.dragonflyministries.com
Illinois

From Theresa Pryor…

I used to pray with the *hope* that God heard my prayers. Over time I realized that God was *answering* my prayers, which showed me that He was *really listening* and that He cared enough about me to respond. I have come to understand that prayer connects us to God. He reveals Himself to us and we gain a greater understanding of Him. Prayer has become a constant in my life. I talk to God about everything. He is my confidant. I have seen people's lives changed through prayer. I have seen people healed of cancer and other illnesses. I have seen people's attitudes changed and I have witnessed miracles happen through prayer. In my darkest times, others have prayed for me and God has pulled me from the depths of despair. *Prayer has transformed my life!*

I continue to pray because it's awesome to see God at work in the lives of others. God can change what we deem impossible and make it possible. I pray for someone, then stand back with anticipation and excitement and watch God work in their lives. There is so much God wants to reveal to us if we would only take time in our day to seek Him. He's waiting to hear from you. He has so much to share with you. Pray and then wait and see what He does in your life!

– Theresa Pryor, Columbus, Ohio

From Peg Buehlman...

Why pray? I used to pray what I'll call "bargain" prayers: Lord, if You fix this I'll.... Then when life got hard I just started being real with God, sharing my fears and failures, and eventually my heart changed. I became more grateful. His unfailing love was changing me. I realized by spending more time with Him that He accepted me and loved me unconditionally. When I started taking the time to listen for His voice, He was there, speaking to my heart. I knew it was Him. It was humbling and awesome all at the same time. I still ponder how my God can want such an intimate relationship with me, but most of the time now I just bask in the wonder of how "How Great Thou Art."

— Peg Buehlman, Ellicott City, MD

READY TO PRAY

Prayer Journal

January

_____
_____
_____
_____
_____
_____
_____
_____
_____
_____
_____
_____
_____
_____
_____
_____
_____
_____
_____
_____
_____
_____
_____
_____

January Prayer Requests

January Praise Reports

February

February Prayer Requests

February Praise Reports

_____

_____

_____

_____

_____

_____

_____

_____

_____

_____

_____

_____

_____

_____

_____

_____

_____

_____

_____

_____

_____

_____

_____

_____

_____

_____

_____

_____

_____

March

_____
_____
_____
_____
_____
_____
_____
_____
_____
_____
_____
_____
_____
_____
_____
_____
_____
_____
_____
_____
_____
_____
_____
_____

March Prayer Requests

March Praise Reports

_____
_____
_____
_____
_____
_____
_____
_____
_____
_____
_____
_____
_____
_____
_____
_____
_____
_____
_____
_____
_____
_____
_____
_____

April

April Prayer Requests

April Praise Reports

May

May Prayer Requests

May Praise Reports

June

June Prayer Requests

June Praise Reports

July

July Prayer Requests

July Praise Reports

August

August Prayer Requests

August Praise Reports

September

September Prayer Requests

September Praise Reports

October

October Prayer Requests

October Praise Reports

November

_____
_____
_____
_____
_____
_____
_____
_____
_____
_____
_____
_____
_____
_____
_____
_____
_____
_____
_____
_____
_____
_____
_____
_____

November Prayer Requests

November Praise Reports

December

December Prayer Requests

December Praise Reports

Prayer Resources

Suggested Books on prayer:

Ready to Pray by Pastor Gail Dudley
A Journey to Victorious Praying by Bill Thrasher
　　(Moody Publishers)
Developing a Prayer-Care-Share Lifestyle
　　(HOPE Ministries)
Fresh Wind, Fresh Fire by Jim Cymbala
Intercessory Prayer by Dutch Sheets
I Told the Mountain to Move by Patricia Raybon
　　(SaltRiver)
Learning to Pray Through the Psalms by James W. Sire
　　(InterVaristy Press)
The Power of a Praying Woman by Stormie Omartian
　　(Harvest House Publishers)
Pray with Purpose, Live with Passion by Debbie Williams
　　(Howard Books)
Prayer by Richard J. Foster (HarperCollins Publishers)
Prayer 101: Experiencing the Heart of God
　　by Warren Wiersbe (Cook Communications)

Praying God's Word by Beth Moore
    (Broadman & Holman Publishers)
Praying with Women of the Bible by Nancy Kennedy
    (Zondervan)
Possessing the Gates of the Enemy by Cindy Jacobs
Prayer Shield by C. Peter Wagner
What Happens When Women Pray by Evelyn Christensen
    (Cook Communications)
Spurgeon on Prayer & Spiritual Warfare
    by Charles Spurgeon
Disciple's Prayer Life by T.W. Hunt & Catherine Walker
How to Hear from God by Joyce Meyer
Possessing the Gates of the Enemy by Cindy Jacobs
Prayers that Avail Much
    by Germaine Copeland World Ministries, Inc.
Beyond the Veil by Alice Smith
Intercessory Prayer by Dutch Sheets
Prayer Shield by C. Peter Wagner
Fasting by Jentezen Franklin
A Hunger for God by John Piper
Intimacy with the Almighty by Charles R. Swindoll

Suggested DVD Series on Prayer:

When God's People Pray by Jim Cymbala

Suggested Study Bibles:

The Power of a Praying Woman Bible (NIV)
      by Stormie Omartian (Harvest House Publishers)

Suggested Workshops:

The 5-Hour Journey of Prayer Instruction is a one day/5-hour journey of prayer instruction designed to equip individuals, groups, and churches that desire to go deeper in their prayer journey as well as to be effective and impactful during prayer gatherings. For details of future conferences, please visit the website: www. GailDudley.com

Ministry in Motion Ministries founder Gail Dudley is available to bring this workshop to you, sowing 10 percent of the profit back into your ministry or church. The cost per person for the conference is $75.00 per person (non-refundable). The cost includes the 215-page workbook. The cost of lunch is not included.

Suggested Websites on Prayer:

http://www.teachmetopray.com/
   (free 52-week online prayer school)
http://www.globaldayofprayer.com/
http://www.presidentialprayerteam.org/
http://www.prayinglife.org/
http://www.allaboutprayer.org/

Suggested Bible Studies on Prayer:

Boldly Asking by Aletha Hinthorn
   (Beacon Hill Press of Kansas City)
Connecting with God from Stonecroft Ministries
Disciple's Prayer Life: Walking in Fellowship with God
   by T.W. Hunt & Catherine Walker
   (LifeWay Church Resources)
Prayer: An Adventure with God by David Healey
   (InterVarsity)

STATEMENT OF FAITH

GOD

We believe in one God, existing as three persons; Father, Son, and Holy Spirit, is the loving Creator of all that is, eternal and good, knowing all things, having all power, and desiring and inviting covenant relationship with humanity *(Matt. 28:19; 1 Tim. 1:17; Heb. 1:1-3; 9:14)*.

JESUS CHRIST

We believe in our Lord Jesus Christ, God manifest in the flesh. He alone is the Savior and Lord, the Son of God and God the Son, born of a virgin, the perfect example of humanity, crucified for the sin of the world, raised on the third day and who lives forever to make intercession for us. We confess the absolute lordship and leadership of the risen Jesus Christ, who is the Son of God and God the Son, and our soon-returning King *(Col. 1:15-20; Col. 2:9; John 1:1; Gal. 4:4; Phil. 3:10)*.

THE HOLY SPIRIT

We believe in God the Holy Spirit. At the point of salvation a person receives the Holy Spirit. We receive the abiding presence, peace, and power of the Holy Spirit in every believer as sufficient and necessary for normal Christian living *(Acts 1:8; Eph. 2:22; Rom. 8:9-30)*.

SCRIPTURE

We believe in the Holy Scripture as originally given by Christ, divinely inspired, and revealed by God, unchanging and infallible Word of God, correct doctrine, the complete truth, authority, and relevance of every promise, provision, God's story of love and redemption (John 1:1; 2 Pet. 1:19-21; 2 Tim. 2:15; 3:16).

SALVATION

We believe in the salvation of the lost and sinful people by grace alone, through faith alone, in Christ alone. We accept the grace of God through the finished work of Jesus on the cross as victory for eternal and abundant life, and we maintain spiritual sonship and citizenship in the present and future Kingdom of God *(Rom. 10:9-10; Eph. 2:8-9)*.

UNITY of THE BODY OF CHRIST

We believe in the unity of the Body of Christ and in the Spirit. Unity comprised of, teaching, prayer, fellowship, breaking of bread, meeting ministry needs, praise and worship, people being saved *(Eph. 4:1-6; Acts 2:42-47)*.

HUMANITY

We celebrate the sacredness and uniqueness of every person as wonderfully created in the image of God and according to God's sovereign will, called to lives of Christlikeness through personal holiness, honor, and humility *(Heb. 2:6-12)*.

SIN and EVIL

We acknowledge our sin and brokenness but refute anything that seeks to deny, discourage, or destroy the life that Jesus offers to all believers *(2 Cor. 4:1-18)*.

MINISTRY

We believe that we should go, preach, and make disciples of Jesus Christ. We believe that we should be a witness for the Lord. We value the fellowship of Christian believers in loving community, gifted service, mutual encouragement and with godly leadership as representative of the presence of Christ on earth to meet the real needs of people *(Matt. 28:19-20; Acts 1:8; Acts 2:41-47)*.

WORSHIP

We affirm that every person is called to glorify the living God completely, freely, and passionately by giving their lives in authentic relationship, their resources in responsible stewardship, and their devotion in faithful discipleship *(Jn. 4:23-24)*.

PRAYER

We believe in communication with God and availability to God to do God's will in the earth. We believe that we must go to God with our heart and come away with His *(Matt.6)*.

ABOUT THE AUTHOR

Gail E. Dudley

"...bringing you closer to Christ."

With a commitment to delivering messages that are both scriptural and applicable to real life situations, Gail E. Dudley shares the words that are spoken into her heart by the Holy Spirit and delivers those messages to the listener's ear.

One of her most rewarding experiences was participating as a conference speaker in Bulawayo, Zimbabwe, Africa, for The Women Unlimited of Word of Life International Annual Conference. Gail serves as a speaker and author with a passion to provide guidance to God's people as they navigate through their spiritual journey.

Currently Gail serves as a pastor at The Church at North Pointe, providing guidance, teaching discipleship studies, and overseeing multiple outreach efforts. She is also the Vice President of Diversity for Stonecroft Ministries, and works actively with the Mission America Coalition.

Gail is the wife of Reverend Dr. Kevin Dudley, senior pastor of The Church at North Pointe (Columbus, Ohio) and the loving mother of Alexander and Dominiq. Gail connects with people where they are in their journey and, upon hearing her speak, it is evident that Gail walks closely with the Lord, spends time daily in the Word, and seeks always to be ready to share God's truth for transforming lives.

BOOKING INFORMATION

If you would like to schedule Gail to speak at your retreat, your book club, or to do a book signing or a reading, please contact, Gail at:

www.GailDudley.com
GED@MIMToday.org
614-441-8178

We would love to hear from you. Send us your testimony and/or prayer request.

TRANSFORMATIONAL WEEKEND RETREATS

In our culture today believers inevitably find themselves living their lives based upon false beliefs, very often unaware of the many harmful influences that have shaped and continue to hold us captive. To experience a life of truth it is absolutely critical to know the truth. God's truth is what sets us free! Many people have the desire to know the truth, but are unsure how to connect and apply God's truth. Just as we do today, the woman in Genesis 3 fell into the serpent's trap, but God gives us all that we need to overcome the lies. During this transformational weekend participants will gain insight that will help to strengthen and inspire us in our walk with the Lord.

If you desire to go deeper in your walk with Christ, this is for you.

If you would like to host a "Transformational Weekend" and have Gail Dudley come to your area, contact Gail at GED@MIMToday.org.

Each "Transformational Weekend" begins on the scheduled Friday at 1:00 p.m. in a time of prayer instruction and inner healing followed by quiet time. Saturday morning beginning at 9:30 we will identify the lies that have been spoken into our life and replace those lies with the truth by asking, "Who Told You That?" The second session on Saturday, "Ready to Change My Name," will position us for transformation.

Our weekend will conclude at 12:30 p.m. with small group instruction that will equip each participant to form small groups and share this teaching with others.

Space is limited. Only seven participants per scheduled weekend retreat. Cost: $125.00 per person ~ includes all sessions and materials. Interesting in learning more about the "Transformational Weekend Retreats?" If you would like to place yourself on the upcoming retreat list or host a "Transformational Weekend Retreat" in your area, contact us at GED@MIMToday.org.

Because there is a demand to have a one-day "Transformational" session, we have put together a seven-hour session. To host or schedule a "Transformational" session, contact Gail at GED@ MIMToday.org.

OTHER BOOKS BY GAIL

Ready to Change My Name ~
A Spiritual Journey from Fear to Faith

Ready to Pray ~
A Spiritual Journey of Praise and Worship

Ready to Pray (30 Minute Prayer CD)

Transparent Moments of Gail Dudley

Who Told You That? ~
The Truth Behind the Lies

ORDER ADDITIONAL COPIES TODAY

Gail E. Dudley
5550 Cleveland Avenue
Columbus, Ohio 43231-4049

Name: _____

Address: _____

City: _____ State: _____ Zip: _____

E-mail: _____

Would you like to join our mailing list? ❑ Yes   ❑ No thank you.

Telephone: (   ) _____ - _____

Ready to Change My Name   qty: _____ ($15.00 each + $2.50 S & H)

Ready to Pray (the Book)   qty: _____ ($15.00 each + $2.50 S & H)

Ready to Pray
(215 page Workbook)   qty: _____ ($24.95 each + $3.50 S & H)

Ready to Pray
(30 Minute Prayer CD)   qty: _____ ($7.00 each + $2.50 S & H)

Who Told You That?   qty:_____ ($17.50 each + $3.00 S & H)

Transparent Moments   qty: _____ ($7.00 each + $3.00 S & H)

Book Total: $ _____   S & H Total: _____ = Grand Total $_____

Number of books being shipped: _____

Please make checks payable to:
Gail E. Dudley

Send payment to:
5550 Cleveland Avenue, Columbus, Ohio 43231-4049

Please allow two (2) weeks for shipping

CPSIA information can be obtained
at www.ICGtesting.com
Printed in the USA
FSOW03n0800040416
18758FS